MW01713734

Praise for Father Leo's Story

Fr. Leo could have written an autobiography and simply recounted his life as a Catholic Priest, but he chose to do much more than that. Instead, he took the time to examine and reflect deeply on his own experiences. What he has gifted us with, is a treasure trove of insight, learnings, unsettling questions, and some disturbing truths. Ultimately, Fr. Leo's greatest gift is the affirmation of God's powerful love embodied in all of creation, and the inspiration to claim our place and power as people of God - to pour "new wine into new wineskins."
Liz Fowler, Retired Catholic School Principal

Fr. Leo is definitely one of a kind in so many interesting ways. Reading through his eyes gives me a better understanding of his passionate drive, and courageous willingness to open our hearts and minds to our own life journey of constant rethinking and relearning. He exposes indifference, apathy, inequality and ambiguity in many areas of our society. I find that his work offers great hope for moving forward after our recent troubling times during Covid-19. "Father Leo's Story" inspires deep reflection.
Colleen Rivers, Retired Teacher

Having known and followed Fr. Leo for over 40 years, I am eagerly awaiting his second book. Fr. Leo is one of those unique people who sees through an incredibly creative and insightful lens, urging himself and others to think deeper and be the "skin" of God. I am sure his story will inspire us, just as his life's work has.
Su Musclow, Retired School Principal

Praise for Father Leo's Story

My wife was raised Roman Catholic, and I was raised Protestant. We have attended an Anglican, and then a United Church, for over 20 years. Both being "wannabe mystics" for almost 50 years, we have been practicing daily meditation, and are avid readers of Richard Rohr and Thomas Keating. During the pandemic lockdown a friend invited us to check out a Zoom Mass celebrated by Father Leo Coughlin. She said he was Canada's Richard Rohr. She was right. Fr. Leo brings the heart of God into all he says and does - from welcoming everyone to the communion table, to championing local social justice causes. He inspired my wife and I to participate in our first ever social justice march for "Every Child Matters" – the campaign recognizing the terrible harm done to Canada's First Nation's children in the residential school system. We are both eager to read his reflections, looking back at his life well-lived.
Mark and Sue Woollard, Brampton, Ontario

Father Leo's Story:

As Seen through the Rearview Mirror

Father Leo's Story:
As Seen through the Rearview Mirror

Cover Art by Yvonne Guerin
Book Design by Stone Circle Press
www.stonecirclepress.com

You can follow Fr. Leo's daily reflections on Facebook at
www.facebook.com/leo.coughlin.7

Library and Archives Canada Cataloguing in Publication

Coughlin, Leo
Father Leo's Story: As Seen through the Rearview Mirror

ISBN: 9798818653129

Dedication

I dedicate this book to my ten siblings, who by loving me inspired me to live a life rich with zeal and humour. I am forever grateful to Rita, Patricia, Richard, Audrey, Barbara, Charlie, Mary, Carmel, Gerry and Shirley.

With gratitude to the exceptional artist Yvonne Guerin who created the painting on the cover, I truly appreciate your artistic ability. Thank you!

CONTENTS

Introduction

I have been on a journey in ministry for 64 years, and have been taught and learned a great deal. I have been educated by nature herself. I grew up loving the land and all she birthed, year after year. I was taught by the people of God to be vulnerable and to accept being love, and from this I learned to love and to serve - excluding no one. Finally, I was taught by the Master. Jesus taught me to give my life away in service, just as he gave his life away. Now as I look back through the rearview mirror, I see that it has been a wonderful and challenging journey. I am so glad that I have walked on the highway of life with so many loving companions! I see anew the manner in which the communion of saints - those who are still with me and those who have moved on - have influenced me. I look back and see the highs and the lows of the journey, but mostly just everyday living filled with challenges, to see and do the will of God. I have drawn on my life experiences, having pondered their meaning and purpose, to write *Fr. Leo's Story: As Seen through the Rearview Mirror*.

Fr. Leo Couglin, May 2022

Chapter 1

A FARMER'S CHILD

The Coughlin Homestead

In 1833 my ancestors came from Ireland, and settled on a 100-acre farm in Asphodel Township, near Peterborough, Ontario. This is where my story begins.

Many years later I was born, and my journey in life began. My family consisted of my father, my mother and ten siblings. I was number nine of eleven, and I had seven sisters (Rita, Patricia, Audrey, Barbara, Mary, Carmel and Shirley) and three brothers (Richard, Charles and Gerry). I was born into poverty during the Great Depression.

Even though life was difficult, we were a happy family. What I remember most, was everyone's playfulness and laughter.

Our community was Irish Catholic, located in St. Paul's Catholic Parish in Norwood, Ontario, Canada. It was the norm that everyone, ourselves and other families, would work on the farm. We all had to work very hard.

When I began school, I attended what was then known as Number 6 Daisy D. School, which was located on the 7th Concession of Asphodel, right beside St. Paul's Cemetery. Living by the Irish way of life, we were a very traditional Catholic family with morning and night prayers, prayers of grace before and after meals, and the rosary every evening. When praying the rosary, some of us were not always attentive. Sometimes we would pinch someone and then get them giggling. We all tried not to make any noise, as there would be big trouble from our father if he caught the culprit.

Eventually my father bought two more farms, one for each of my older brothers, Richard and Charles, and my youngest brother Gerry, was to inherit the homestead. I could see the handwriting on the wall, that I was not getting a farm. I still remember the day when I was about 13 years old, on a hot July day working in the hay field, when it suddenly hit me. I announced to my two brothers, "I am not going to be a farmer, it's too much work, too many hours, and too demanding." I thought that I would leave the farm, go to the city, get a much easier job, and work only 35 hours a week. Many years later, that is exactly what I did.

I spent four years, Grades 9 through 12, in Norwood High School. Then for Grade 13 I attended St. Michael's School in Toronto. After graduating, I got a job in Toronto. I rode a streetcar to and from work every day, and worked 35 hours each week. I really did not know what to do with my life. I prayerfully pondered the question, "How can I spend my life to be useful and meaningful?"

Eventually a feeling arose in my heart, that I was being called by God to the Priesthood. I did not like this. Strange as it may seem, I did not admire Priests.

I saw them wearing long black dresses and frilly tops, and working only one day a week. This did not appeal to me. However, the urge became stronger and stronger until I made a pact with God, that I would go to the Seminary for two years, and then leave and get a real job.

I did register at St. Augustine's Seminary. I made the long seven year's journey, and only at the end of the seventh year, did I remember I had only intended to stay for two years. I was ordained a Priest on May 31, 1958, and said my first Mass on June 1, 1958 in St. Paul's Church at Norwood, which was our family Parish.

Pastoral Reflection

When I was a teenager my heart's desire was to earn a lot of money, buy the good life, and live happily ever after. As I look back over my formative years, I realize that for the most part my childhood was a happy one. Yes, there were struggles with poverty and hardship, but I also belonged to a very caring family, a family of strong faith and full of love. Every evening before bedtime my father, who had promised his mother that every day he would pray with his family, led us in the family rosary. I learned very early that prayer had to be an important part of my spiritual life. I also learned the meaning of working with a commitment. This has been of great value to me in my years of ministry.

I never had to wait to be told to do something. Like my father and mother, I was a self-starter able to put in a full day's work, not just a couple of hours. The other big lesson I learned from my family was to have consideration for the well-being of other people. My father and mother were an example and an inspiration. I have tried to be present and helpful to other people who are struggling.

I internalized the importance of laughter and play. There always seemed to be much laughter around the dinner table in our home, practical jokes and humor. It seemed that every member of our family was a comedian.

I have kept this up over my lifetime, as I really enjoy laughing and telling jokes. I do not do practical jokes anymore. Playing was so important to us! How often I heard my parents say, “Kids - go outside and play.” This got us out of the house, and they had some peace and quiet. From this I was taught to keep playing, that life is to be enjoyed, and to find happiness in that enjoyment.

Finally, my family taught me the importance of being a good neighbor. In a farming community being a good neighbor was extremely important. When a neighbor needed assistance from time to time, other neighbors showed up to help. As a Priest and living in a Parish, I did not see the people as parishioners. I saw them as neighbors and friends, and as I have a good memory, I memorized each one so I could greet them by name. I carried this ability on into my Parishes. Then on Sundays while serving the Eucharist, I was able to call people by their name, and to know how important that was to them.

As I reflect on growing up in my Irish Catholic family, I hope you can see how I was shaped by the forces of the culture that I was immersed in. My family certainly set me on a road for the living of life, in the manner of which I would continue. It is true to say that I am grateful for what my family gave me, and for what my faith community gave me. This all played a big role in creating the person that I am today, and for that I am grateful to all. I thank God for placing me in my family and in my community.

Deo Gratias

Chapter 2

STILL A FARMER'S CHILD

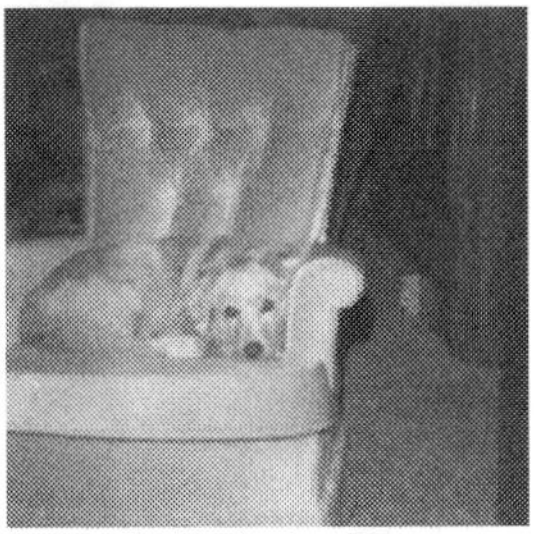

Fr. Leo's dog Tina

As I reflect on my journey, I realize I am a country boy - nothing more and nothing less. I attended high school in Norwood, and it was probably the unhappiest time of my life. I just never seemed to fit in. The fact that I lived in the country made it hard to visit with the kids in town, and I believe that this played a huge role in not being able to develop deep friendships. It was when I was in grade 10 that my father died in an accident. My mother was left with 7 kids still at home, and a failing farm business that was still feeling the effects of the Great Depression.

She took hold of the business, and it soon became profitable. Then slowly but surely, my sisters began to leave home and head to Toronto for a career and a boyfriend. The following is a story about the "boyfriend."

When my sisters brought a boyfriend home from Toronto to introduce to the family, my little brother Gerry and I would introduce him to the farm. We offered to show him around, and took him out to the barn and fields to teach him about farming, with him wearing city shoes and fancy trousers. We had to walk across the barnyard, stepping on cow pies all the way. Gerry and I were wearing boots and were fully aware of how best to walk around these obstacles. But for the "boyfriend," you can imagine what this did to the shiny shoes and the legs of the trousers. Not pretty!

One of the tricks I remember best was taking the boyfriends out one by one, to show them what an electric fence was, and how it worked. On the chance that someone does not know what an electric fence is, it is simply a wire strung from post to post with an electric battery attached to the wire. The concept is, that the cows will touch the wire, get a shock, back off and stay in the pasture. I remember taking those city slickers out to show them the electric fence, and I would show them that you could touch it and not get a shock. The secret was to close your hand over the wire, and you would be safe. When it was the boyfriend's time to touch the wire I said, "Just stretch out your fingers and touch the wire." They saw me do it and they believed me. They did stretch out their fingers and touch the wire, but naturally they got a shock and landed on their backside. I did not tell them you had to close your hand, in order not to get a shock! There were many other tricks Gerry and I played on them. Needless to say, many of the boyfriends never returned to visit the farm a second time.

When I was in Grade 12, the school curriculum included the Inquisition and the Crusades. The teacher was a devout Presbyterian, and he certainly wanted the class to know the dark side of the Catholic Church. As a Catholic, I was in the minority.

When he continued to teach these topics to the students, I found myself slipping lower and lower into my desk. I was embarrassed by the material that was presented, and to learn what rotten people Catholics were.

This was all news to me. I had never heard of it before, and was caught unaware. As I previously said, along with other reasons my high school days are best forgotten. The only reason I went to school was to get away from working on the farm.

Pastoral Reflection

As I look back on my high school years, I still find them painful and embarrassing. Part of my embarrassment was because I did not know anything about the Crusades, the Inquisition, or other Catholic histories. This was the first time I had attended a school where Catholic and Protestant students were in the same classroom. Until that point in my life I did not know any Protestants, and did not know anything about their beliefs or way of life. Despite this, we intermingled, made good friends and learned to respect each other's faith community.

Unfortunately, living four miles away meant a long walk to and from school, and a longer walk if we wanted to meet up with friends for fun. Back in Grade 8 I was hired as the caretaker of my elementary school. I had to go early in the morning to start the fire, so the school would be warm when the other students arrived. Also sweeping the school was part of my duties, and for this I was paid all of $8.00. With that money in my pocket I went into Peterborough with my father, and bought a used bicycle. This became a lifesaver to me, for the four years that I was at Norwood High.

As I reflect on those years in High School I see that I was reluctant to stand up and defend myself. I have always held that there must have been something good about the Crusades and the Inquisition, yet to this day I do not know what that good might have been.

I still remember the fact that on Sundays I would be visiting with friends in the village, and later in the afternoon would have to go home and milk the cows, while my friends spent the day together.

It was during those times that I really detested being a farmer. It is ironic that the 24/7 life of a farmer, which I hated, eventually became my life as a Priest. Living in a house attached to the Church meant that I was always on duty. I left the farm to avoid 24/7 and ended up in a ministry that was 24/7!

I also remember that I grew up with a deep love for the Earth. I really enjoyed working in the fields with the tractor, and cultivating the Earth. I remember one day when I was in the field with my father, and he picked up a handful of Earth. Holding it in his hand, he showed it to me and said, "Son, if you take care of the Earth, the Earth will take care of you." I have never forgotten that teaching, and it reinforced my love for the Earth, for all living creatures, for animals, and especially for all people. It is amazing how one small teaching can open our hearts! The love of the Earth has always been a solid energy in my life, and emerges in a form of curiosity and attention to creation. For me, creation is one of the best teachers in the presence and action of God in everyday life.

At 17 years of age, I left home to go to Toronto to make my fortune. I soon found out that there was no money tree in Toronto. For a year I worked for a company there, and during this time I lived with my sister Barbara and her husband Bud. It was during this time that as I knelt by my bed at night to say my prayers, slowly but surely my vocation became known to me. A small voice within told me I was called to the Priesthood. In the beginning, I just wanted to silence that little voice. I did not like Priests and did not want to be one. As the year went on, the voice became stronger and stronger, and eventually wore down my resistance.

I returned to Peterborough, met with the Bishop, and made arrangements to attend Saint Augustine Seminary in Toronto.

After seven years of study, I was ordained to the Priesthood on May 31, 1958.

Now 64 years later I am completing the journey, bringing it to closure. It has been an interesting passage, and an adventure with many highs and lows. I will reveal more in the pages that follow.

Deo Gratias

Chapter 3

ST. AUGUSTINE'S SEMINARY, HERE I COME

St. Paul's Church, Norwood, ON

In September 1951, I found myself registered at Saint Augustine Seminary in Scarborough, Ontario. As I arrived, I realized that I was starting to keep my promise. But remember, I did not want to be a Priest! I really was not fond of Priests, so I made a deal with God that I would go to the Seminary for two years, and then I would leave, get a real career and make lots of money. My desire for a lot of money was a strong motivation.

Slowly, my life became one with Seminary life. In the Seminary there were over 200 young men. It was a strange kind of lifestyle. The hour of every day began with a bell ringing, that was called "the voice of God."

Thus began my journey into the future. At the end of my two years I had forgotten about my agreement with God, and returned to the Seminary for my third year.

Eventually I returned for my seventh year and was ordained to the Priesthood on May 31, 1958.

It was a strange life in the Seminary, almost like being in prison. There were no newspapers, no radio, no television, no leaving the property except at Christmas and summer holidays when we could go home. It was like a lockdown. However, I quickly made friends with five other young men and together we moved forward. Unfortunately, one by one, each decided not to continue the journey, and all left for home. Every time one of them left, it was a sad day for me. In my fourth year I found a whole new life, when I started to study theology. I read books on theology to learn more and more about God, and the ways of God.

There was moral theology, dogmatic theology, acetic theology, spiritual formation, and finally canon law. Canon law was my fit, and on my exams I always scored in the 90's. I often wondered why I excelled at Canon law. The joke was to know Canon law, so we would know what laws to break when we became a Priest! The other thing I remember about my time in the Seminary was the lack of food. I was always hungry.

All in all, there were many things about Seminary life that I enjoyed. Over the years I made many friends, there was always companionship, and the daily routine and the studies filled our days. I found the study of St. Thomas Aquinas to be extremely enriching, and thus wholeheartedly embraced it. Only later when I discovered the emerging new faith story, did I have to change my mind about many things. The one was to **know** God, and not just to know **about** God.

Pastoral Reflection

As I look back over the seven years in the Seminary, I realize in many ways they were years of growth and transformation. They were years in which I learned many skills, and developed good relationships with my class-mates.

It was in the Seminary where many of my questions, and much of my curiosity, was satisfied. I now see, that I was not really prepared to go out into the world and minister to people in a Parish. My professors, all good men, never worked in a parish so were not able to give any real strategies on ministering to the people of God. It was learning by experience, watching other Priests in their ministry, and making mistakes. Slowly but surely, I grew in maturity, and developed the ability to step outside of the box in order to properly minister to Parishioners.

One of the things I lost in Seminary life was spontaneous prayer. Before I attended the seminary, I was a man who loved nature, and it was in nature that I experienced the Divine. It was in nature that I felt close to God, and God close to me. It was in nature that I experienced a deep and abiding peace, that made me feel content and happy. In the seminary, prayer was pretty much by rote. We memorized prayers both individually and collectively. For meditation we had a book in which we read a paragraph, and there were five questions which we had to think about, and somehow make sense out of the reading. It did not work for me, as I was used to silence and stillness to be in touch with the divine. I lost the prayer of silence, as being immersed in rote praying for so long I forgot how to spend quiet time in silence. Only later did I realize that silence is the language of God. It was several years after ordination that I went back to praying and stillness, and using the language of God, which is silence.

Yes, in that silent time I experienced the presence and love of God, and peace which is truly a gift of God.

It was during those years in the seminary toward the end of my seventh year when I stepped up and stepped out vocally, and in my actions found I had the self-confidence and ability to act on my own. During the seven years I spent in the seminary I was never asked to help, or appointed any kind of duties. When an opportunity arose to be responsible for replacing light bulbs in the chapel, I volunteered and got the job.

Another friend joined me in this responsibility. It was a funny job because I had never paid attention to the lighting in the Chapel, and suddenly word came from on high reminding me that the lights in the Chapel needed attention. This would happen twice a year and worked well for me, as having this particular job relieved me of being asked to do anything else. On the one hand I felt left out, but on the other I was glad I had volunteered to replace the lightbulbs in the Chapel.

As I reflected on my time in the Seminary, I realized the grace time that it was. Companionship was rich with good friends, good conversation, good jokes, and plenty of laughter. The regular time for prayer prepared me to live a life of prayer, although quite different from what I learned in the Seminary. I had to let it go, and replace it with daily meditation. As already mentioned, I was faced with a theology that was outdated, a theology that had developed in the Middle Ages and did not fit the world of 1958-59. I became a lifelong learner. On the one hand, I found that I had the right kind of mind for psychology, and as a result twice a year I would go away to a seminar where the topic was psychology. I bought and read many books on psychology. Eventually I returned to university in Ottawa and obtained an M.A. in psychology. Next, I engaged in spiritual reading. New authors were bringing forward new ideas, new ways of looking at the world, new ways of opening my eyes, and new ways for seeing the presence and action of God. As a result of psychology and my developing spirituality, I found myself to be more flexible when ministering to the people of God.

As previously said, I stepped out of the box and as a result was able to be more flexible, more responsive, and more pastoral. The overriding motive in my life was to put people first, and rise above law and rules. I remember my first Mass on June 1, 1958. There was a quiet moment, and I heard a voice from within me say, "Father Leo I want you to always put people first." At the time I had no idea what that could mean, and I had to discover this directive through experience over the years.

Soon after ordination I could see that the Church had become very legalistic, and keeping the law was extremely important, even if it meant that people were refused God. This did not sit well with me. I felt my Ministry was to respond to the people's need with love, compassion and kindness, not to be stopped or prevented by some law or rule. For the past fifty years I have tried to put people first, no matter what was going on in their lives. It may be an addiction, something criminal, depression or anxiety, the ending of a marriage, the inability to lovingly parent children, or whatever the situation - I put people first. By bringing them love and compassion I could help them to make better decisions for themselves and their family. My training in psychology has been a real blessing for many people because psychology removed me from criticism or judgement, and removed from my mind any sense of superiority, or that I had it all together.

Many times I got into trouble with the "powers that be." Sometimes other Priests reported me to the Bishop of the day, and he would call me in to reprimand me. I let him talk but I knew that I was not going to change. I was going to put people first - no matter what the cost to me. Even today, with over 60 years of Ministry behind me I still put people first, because I feel it was the words of the Holy Spirit that were spoken within my heart, on the day I presided at my first Holy Mass.

I know it has caused me a lot of pain, betrayal by some friends, and reprimands by Bishops. However, some people have come back to say thank you - only a very few - but that is okay. I decided for my own mental health that I would not take offence, or create any self-imposed repression, or feel anger, or a desire to blame or get even.

Deo Gratias

Chapter 4

LIFE IN THE NORTH Part 1

On a beautiful summer day, I was ordained into the Priesthood by the late Bishop Webster. On June 1, 1958 I joined with family and friends to preside at my first Mass in St. Paul's Church in Norwood. It was during that Mass that as I paused for a moment, I heard a voice say, "Father Leo, I want you to put people first." In September I was assigned to St. Peter's Parish in Parry Sound. I remember a dark and cloudy Saturday afternoon driving north with my brother Charles, so I could take up residence there.

This was the beginning of a long and arduous journey of four years. The ecosystem was filled with rocks, trees and lakes. It took me years to feel comfortable in that environment. Also, it took me some time to find the Church, by that I mean a faith community that was Catholic.

I came from an Irish Catholic community, and now was taking up residence in a community made up of Francophones, Dutch, Czechoslovakian, Ukrainian and First Nations. This was news to me, and a big adjustment was ahead of me. Within a year I felt quite comfortable in my home away from home. There was no Catholic school in the Parish, yet the Priests ahead of me had established a very successful Baltimore catechism program.

The people knew that catechism very well, and it was the basis of their faith lifestyle. They had been taught and had come to believe in a God who judged the living and the dead, and the existence of purgatory and hell (and if you were lucky, heaven). There was also a belief in limbo, where the unbaptized babies supposedly went. St. Peter's had two missions - one in Nobel about 10 miles north of Parry Sound, and one in Mactier, about 25 miles south of Parry Sound. That was my run every Sunday. I would drive to Nobel for 9:00 am Mass which was held in the community hall, where a dance had been held the Saturday night before. When the dance was finished everyone went home, so no one cleaned the hall. On Sunday morning, with the help of a parishioner, we would clean the hall, pack away the empty beer bottles, empty the ashtrays and somehow get some fresh air into the space. When Mass was finished, I would drive back to Parry Sound, and then on to Mactier for 11:00 am Mass. I really came to love the people of Mactier, they were extremely kind to me. In the four years I drove that road during great snowstorms, I never missed a Sunday. Sometimes I was the only person on Highway 69, yet I was confident I could arrive safely.

Pastoral Reflection

There are a couple of incidents that stick in my mind, as I reflect on those four years in Parry Sound. I had been there for about four months when the phone rang late one night, and it was the hospital calling. At that time the hospital was administered and staffed by the Sisters of St. Joseph. A Sister on the phone told me it was an emergency, and I was needed at the hospital immediately. I got dressed and drove to the hospital, wondering what the emergency was. When I got in the door, I was told to go to the maternity ward where a young woman had just given birth to a baby and the baby had died. As I went into the room, I saw the woman lying on the bed and she was distraught, absolutely heartbroken. She had so looked forward to the coming of her baby and had wonderful thoughts of caring for her child. As I sat on a chair by her bed, I held her hand and she poured out her story.

She told me how she had enjoyed her pregnancy, having hope and optimism for the future and growth of her child. Then she told me that not only was her child dead, but also that it had not been baptized. She had learned in her catechism class that an unbaptized baby would go to limbo, and that even when she got to heaven, she would never see her baby. These thoughts were tearing her apart even more than the death of the baby. By holding her hand and listening to her pain, she poured out her grief, loss and heartache.

Then I began to console her. I told her that God was with her, and prayed that God would give her the courage and healing to face her future. I told her that there had been a big change in the thinking of the Catholic Church, and that limbo no longer existed. So therefore her child would now be resting in the arms of God, and experiencing God's unconditional love. I told her that when she went to the arms of God, she would meet her baby and it would be a good and glorious day for her. This gave her great comfort and consolation. When I left her room to go home, she was relaxed, at peace and sound asleep.

I arrived home and reflected on my experience. I remember how in the seminary I was taught the existence of limbo, and on my final exam I had to answer a question about limbo and unbaptized children. Suddenly the light went on in my head, and I realized that I had just cancelled limbo! In the moment as I held her hand and felt her pain, I knew I had to give her something to restore her hope and give her comfort. I remembered that in the scripture it said that Jesus was moved by compassion, and not always by what was legal. I realized in that moment I had just imitated Jesus in my own ministry. Still reflecting on my conundrum, I realized that I had ministered to her, out of my compassion, a love that would be healing, comforting, and give her peace. I never had any regrets about being the first to cancel limbo. This was the beginning of a life of pastoral care, which has been my way all these years.

The second thing I remember was driving on Highway 69 - a highway that had many rock cuts.

If you had the misfortune of going into the ditch, your chances of survival were slim. One Sunday as I returned to Parry Sound from Mactier, I came upon a car accident. The driver had missed a curve, and hit a rock face. As I approached the wrecked car, what I saw totally rocked me. At the time, I had only been out of the Seminary for six months, and had never seen a serious car accident. The one I saw that day was bad. The car was wrecked, and there were six bodies lying in the ditch. This was before cell phones, and it was clear that I needed help. Luckily another driver came along and stopped. I asked him to go to the restaurant down the road and call the police and ambulance. Very quickly they arrived and took charge. Even today, I can see that accident - the six bodies lying in the ditch - and remember how helpless I felt. When I finally got home to the rectory, the first thing I did to cheer myself and to help me deal with that sad situation, was to have a good stiff drink.

It was certainly one of the most traumatic experiences of my life. It really reminded me of the fragility of life, how suddenly and quickly it can come to an end. At the time I thought of what a tragic event it was, for the families of those six men. They were all from Sudbury, and were headed to Toronto for a conference. They never made it. At home there would be a wife and children, who had lost their husband and father. I wondered about the wives who would now be alone to raise their families, and how the children would make out in life without a father. This was just one of the many traumatic events that I experienced while in Parry Sound.

This tragic experience helped me to grow, and educated me about accidents and heartaches. It taught me how to exercise pastoral ministry, when families are heartbroken and living with the mystery of sudden death, without any concrete answer. All tragic deaths helped me to mature. I learned the importance of compassion in the face of terrible pain, and to trust a loving God. I have grown in courage, to go to the places where few have had the opportunity and privilege. I have learned to see God, and to trust the spirit to give me moral courage and a compassionate heart.

Chapter 5

LIFE IN THE NORTH Part 2

The Joy of Playing Hockey

I am reminded of a funny episode that happened at St. Joseph's Hospital in Parry Sound. The hospital was staffed by the Peterborough Sisters of St. Joseph, along with a lay staff of doctors and nurses. It was a good little hospital, and certainly carried a great reputation. One of the nurses, a beautiful blonde, came from Europe and was acclimatizing herself to Canadian culture and language. This was a very steep learning curve, especially when you were working as a nurse in a hospital.

One day a ball team came from South River to play in Parry Sound. On the way home there was a car accident, and one of the young men ended up in St. Joseph's Hospital where this nurse worked. Looking back, I could see the chemistry between the two of them, and they became lovebirds. Parry Sound has a nice little golf course, so one day I headed there for a game, and as I was driving back into town I saw the two lovebirds walking along the street hand-in-hand. I thought, I will stop and have a visit with them. I did. We stood on the sidewalk for about half an hour shooting the breeze and talking about one thing or another. Suddenly I heard the young nurse say, "My gosh, you are Father Leo!" My response was, "Why did it take you so long to recognize me?"

"Well," she said, "Back in my country, Priests always wear a black suit and white collar, and you are dressed in a T-shirt and a pair of jeans. I have never seen a Priest dressed like that, so it took me a moment to recognize you." "Well," I said, "I am glad you recognized me because we have known each other for four or five months, and I don't want to be a mystery to you." I said a friendly goodbye, got in my car and drove home.

The next day I decided to do my pastoral visit at the hospital, and was dressed in a black suit with a white collar. I started to make my rounds visiting the sick. I came to a four-bed ward, and in each of the beds there was a man. I walked in and saw the young nurse standing there doing some work. I called out to her saying, "Hello, how are you today?" She turned to look at me, and then she said, "Oh, it's you Father Leo, I recognize you today with your clothes on!" At that point my mind began to race. I wondered what the men would think when they heard words like that! Saying I was embarrassed is an understatement. I started to wonder what those men would tell their families when they got home, and what story was going to be circulating around the people of Parry Sound. I felt like quickly turning around and getting out of that ward as fast as I could!

Pastoral Reflection

As I reflect on that happening, I realize that I learned a lot about myself that would help me to become a better person. When I went away to study psychology a friend of mine said to me, "If you can identify and learn your projections, it will be a growth in your humanity and your relationships." I had been projecting my projections onto other people. Assumptions were simply projections of my own, which I was casting onto them. In the study of psychology, I came to recognize, identify, and name some of my projections. I had a supervisor who watched my growth very closely, and he often pointed out one of my projections. A projection is something about one's own self that we do not recognize, do not know, do not want to know, and is hidden from our sight.

It is in coming to know our own self, our own thoughts, our assumptions and feelings that we reject, and then project onto other people. Projections can cause a lot of trouble, because the result is much negativity which is then projected onto people. We are asking them to carry our projections. This kind of behavior places a great deal of stress on friendships. It creates a lot of anxiety and fear, and in the end it contributes to judgment and discrimination. When I read the Gospels, I realize that Jesus did not project negativity on to other people. He spoke the truth in love. He was able to accept people and love people just as they were, without any kind of judgment or put downs. Jesus was free in his relationships with people, and he was able to nurture them and call forth the best in them. If we want to do the same, we have to identify our projections. We need to see our projections, and recognize that we have power over them. In many ways projections become a sign of an unexamined life. I remember reading that Plato said, "An unexamined life is one not worth living."

Over the years I have been called to minister to many people, including different ethnicities, religions, cultures, and the rich or the poor. There has been freedom to welcome everyone into my circle, and to minister to people without any kind of negativity. Needless to say, I still have a long way to go. The person I am today is much more accepting, and less judgmental or critical. I think the young nurse in St. Joseph's Hospital in Parry Sound who spoke the words "I recognize you today with your clothes on," has been a strong motivation for me to work with, and deal with my projections. To accept my projections and diminish them as much as I can, is to enjoy the freedom of letting go of judgment and criticism. It is one of the fruits of dealing with projections, and being aware of my own experience has been more than worthwhile for me. I have experienced greater freedom in my relationships with people.

Deo Gratias

Chapter 6

MY RETURN TO PETERBOROUGH

The Joy of Playing Softball

After four years in Parry Sound, I was very frustrated with my role as a Priest. Most of my time was spent saying Mass, and any mention of adult education was quickly resisted by the people. They learned the Baltimore Catechism, and were quite satisfied with living that form of Christianity. One of my duties was to take a midnight train to the French River to say Mass, which I did every month, then to catch the midnight train back to Parry Sound. One September day I got a boat ride down the river to Highway 69, and from there I had to hitchhike to the train station. As I stood there in the rain hoping for a ride, I became aware of how disappointed and discouraged I was with my role in the Diocese. There were very few cars on the road. So, feeling very sorry for myself, I made up my mind that if I had to spend another year in this Parish, I would leave the Priesthood. That tells you how down I felt.

Eventually a car stopped and gave me a ride home. A week later, I was informed that I was being transferred to Sacred Heart of Jesus Parish in Peterborough. The day I picked up that transfer was one of the happiest days of my life. In early September I arrived in Peterborough, and saw a living, faith-filled, committed group of people who loved their Parish and identified with it.

As the saying goes, "You never left Sacred Heart, and if you moved you took Sacred Heart with you." The Pastor of Sacred Heart was an elderly man who had paid his dues. He administered the Parish, but did very little Parish work, which created a great void I was happy to fill. In those days the Mass was celebrated in Latin. We had a tremendous Mass choir that produced spirit-filled and uplifting music. The Church was full three times on Sunday morning. It was a Parish that by its way of living, defined a faith community. The people knew one another, as they had lived in the Parish for several generations. They interacted with, and supported one another. Anytime there was a service in the Church, you could guarantee it would be filled. I established myself as a bit of an athlete, and as a result was invited to join the Recreation Committee of the City. I was also on the Board of Big Brothers and Big Sisters. I spent as much time at City Hall as I did in the Church.

There was the care of two hospitals, St. Joseph's and Civic. There were many young people in the Parish, so I started a CYO (Catholic Youth Organization). The Regis Club was already alive and thriving for young adults. My Sundays were very full, with three Masses in the morning, baptisms after lunch, and the CYO meeting and Regis Club after supper. Many young men and women met at the Regis Club, fell in love, became engaged and got married. In those days many assistants did not get along with the Pastor. However, I got along just fine with him. When I was transferred next, he told me how much he loved me. I was surprised to be told by a man that he loved me, but it made me feel grateful to that wonderful Priest. After eight years at Sacred Heart the Bishop transferred me to Immaculate Conception Parish, where I stayed for two years. In 1970, I was transferred to St. Anne's Parish in the north end of Peterborough.

Pastoral Reflection

As I look back on those years of ministry in Sacred Heart Parish, I realize how much people taught me. It was a great time for me, as I really felt I was living a life of purpose and meaning.

As well as preaching at Sunday Masses, I would spend four hours on Saturday in the confessional booth, because in those days people believed that going to confession was important. When I was a kid growing up there was not much time for playing sports, but now in Peterborough there were two arenas five minutes away from Sacred Heart. As a result, I was able to play hockey six times a week. Then in the summer there was a ball league which I enjoyed, and in fact played the position of catcher.

While playing these sports I met a lot of people who became fast friends, and I still have some of these friendships today. When we meet, we tell stories of playing sports at the arenas and ball fields. Those were really very special moments. Today when I meet someone who lived at Sacred Heart Parish, it is as if we had never been separated by 50 years. So many people became my friends.

It was my habit to take a coffee break at 10:00 am. At that time there were no Tim Horton's, so I would go to a parishioner's house, knock on the door, walk in and be welcomed, experience more hospitality, and then a free coffee and good conversation! It was that kind of a parish.

After eight years when the time came for my transfer, and to leave Sacred Heart, I realized how much I was loved by the parishioners. We had a great relationship. I had journeyed with them, saw their struggles, prayed with their sick and dying, went to the cemetery with them, and prayed as we lowered the casket into the grave. After the cemetery, we would return to the parish hall for the reception. This was a great opportunity to visit the family members, and speak words of comfort and hope as they grieved the death of a loved one.

I have the memory of a beautiful Saturday morning in July, sitting on the veranda of Sacred Heart rectory. I was drinking a ginger ale, and Bishop Webster was drinking a coffee. I asked him if he was prepared for the meeting of the Bishops at the Vatican Council.

He asked me what I wanted to see come out of the Council. I said to him, "I don't much care, but there is one thing that has to happen, and that is to get rid of the Latin in the Mass and the Sacraments, and use the vernacular English." Bishop Webster replied to me, "Now, now, Father Leo that will never happen, Latin has been with us too long to get rid of it, that would not be appropriate." My response was, "Bishop, I hope you will join the other Bishops in voting for the end of the Latin and use English liturgies." The Holy Spirit must have been having a good day, when the Bishops voted for the vernacular!

It was a sad day when I left Sacred Heart Parish. I loved that Parish so deeply, and I gave them my life and service. As I drove across the City to Immaculate Conception Parish, I thanked God for bringing me to Sacred Heart, and allowing me the freedom to experiment and grow in pastoral ministry. That growth served me well, as I moved on to new ministries in other Parishes. I thank God for the experience. After that I was sent to Douro, a small parish but a delightful one. Everything was good there, and it was there that I celebrated my 25th Anniversary. My family arranged a dinner that followed Mass. I remember so well what a wonderful dinner the CWL put on for us in the hall!

Deo Gratias

Chapter 7

ON THE MOVE AGAIN

In 1970 I was Director of Adult Education for the Diocese, and working at Immaculate Conception Parish. It was a good life and a good ministry. I spent such a short time there, that it is hard to write much about that time. It was a well-established Parish with very dedicated workers and helpers - friendly people I got to know.

One day Bishop Morocco, a man I greatly admired, called me into his office and said, "Father Leo, would you like to be the Pastor of St. Anne's Parish?" The strange thing was, that I had told my Adult Education Committee I did not want to be a Pastor. Not wanting to be a Parish Priest, actually meant not wanting to be assigned to the boondocks. The idea of being Pastor of a City Parish was different, so I grabbed this offer without any further thinking. I said to Bishop Morocco, "Yes, yes, and yes." In 1970 I moved to St. Anne's Parish as Pastor. Ordinarily a young Priest would serve time in the country, and if he did not screw up, he might get a Parish in the city. I guess Bishop Morocco liked me.

This was a tumultuous time in the Church. The Vatican Council with all of its recommendations, was like dropping a bomb on the Church. It was, "throw out the old and bring in the new." The vast majority of people at St. Anne's were my age - 40 years old - which is still young by today's standards. The next eight years of my life certainly were one of the highlights of my long journey in my ministry. I had studied all the documents of Vatican Council II and was well informed. I thought we needed to be faithful to the Council. The first thing we were instructed to do, was establish a Parish Council. The Vatican Council mandated that a parish would have a Parish Council, but it could only be advisory. I liked the idea of a Parish Council, but I did not like the idea of the Pastor having veto powers. I told the people I would respect and honor any decisions they made, and would never use my veto power. As a result, we worked outside the box, and "creativity" was the word of the day. The parish flourished.

In the beginning there was only three Masses on Sunday. Within two years we had moved up to five Masses every weekend, and the Church was filled at every Mass. 2,500 people came every weekend, and over 500 people were involved in various ministries. Parishioners were involved in the community. They served their parish, served their city, and were very involved in the Third World, especially Jamaica. Parishioners went to Jamaica, and people from Jamaica came to St. Anne's. They wanted to meet the people who were so kind and generous to them.

There were two large Catholic schools in the Parish - St. Anne's and St. Paul's. Many of the teachers were involved in various ministries in the Parish, and this gave a wonderful witness to the students. The Bishop assigned two more Priests as Assistants. We had a great working team, for the good of the people and the glory of God.

I really enjoyed being Pastor, and serving God's people in the Parish. The first thing I did, was to memorize the names of all the parishioners, so when they came to receive Communion I would call them by name.

I made sure I knew where everyone lived. It was a very busy life. I played pick-up hockey, joined in picnics at the lake, and regularly visited the schools and hospitals. It was rather ironic that I had left farm living as it was too much work 24/7, and yet here at St. Anne's my job was 24/7! Those were great years. I thank the people of the Parish as we journeyed together, brought Vatican Council alive, and shaped the Parish into a wonderful place of worship and faithful community. I particularly liked the weekends when 2,500 people came to the Masses, and while it was a lot of work, their faith and love energized me. When I finished on Sunday evenings, I always felt very good.

Pastoral Reflection

When I look back on my eight years as Pastor of St. Anne's I realize that I grew a great deal, as a result of ministering to the people of the Parish. My heart and soul were nurtured by the deep strong faith of the people. They were not easy years, because of all the changes in the Church. I came to hate the word "change." It seemed that every time I brought about a change mandated by Vatican Council, people got angry at me, and some of them would even leave the Parish. Of course, when they went to the next Parish, the Pastor there was making the same changes. While the majority of people were open and willing to cooperate, to go forward in implementing the demands of the Council, there were others who were upset and angry (which is normal). It was during that time when I received hate mail, and some of this mail appeared in the collection plate written on the Sunday bulletin. Thank God for my secretary because she would just throw these bulletins into the garbage!

The Sunday before there was going to be a change, I would announce this to the people, and explain what the meaning was behind the change. I always had the hope that they would understand and willingly accept it. One of the changes we had to initiate, was to install lay readers for the Sacred Scriptures, and women could be part of this. I remember the first Sunday that lay people, men and women, acted as Eucharistic Ministers.

For 600 years, Catholics were told that only the Priest could touch the Eucharist, so it was quite a shock for some of them to see lay women or men fulfilling this role. I could feel the tension in the Church that day. However, soon what had been a shock became normal. I quickly learned that I had to be patient and non-judgmental of people. I really did feel compassion for those who found it difficult to accept the changes taking place, as it was going against everything they held dear. I did learn to be forgiving to the people who wrote the hate mail. Most mail was anonymous. However, because I knew the speech patterns of people, I knew who wrote the hate letters. The other thing I learned was not to make decisions based on popularity. On the one hand, being sensitive to where people were at in their lives, and on the other there was a sense of growth and movement forward in the life of the Church. Therefore, it was a real balancing act for me.

Due to the fact that many of the couples in the Parish were young, the numbers of baptisms grew until we had up to twenty babies to baptize once a month on Sunday afternoon. In my ministry this gave me great joy, to see the love of the children's parents as they gazed at their beautiful babies. Then, to baptize them and welcome them into the Church, and by the grace of the Sacrament prepare them for their journey of faith. It was the kind of joy in my ministry that I fondly look back on. As I baptized these babies, I always hoped and prayed that life would be kind to them. I prayed that they would come to know God and God's unconditional love for them. I hoped that when they attended school, they would be taught that they were God's beloved, not sinners. Over the years I saw many Catholics who struggled with having been taught through Sunday homilies that they were sinners. It was a terrible thing to do to people. They were good people who were simply trying to live life as best they could. I always believed that people should be taught that God is with them, that God loves them unconditionally, and that they are God's beloved. I now see that as they were growing, the people in the Parish were teaching me about life, teaching me about God's presence and God's unconditional love.

Certainly I now see the power in the passage, “It is in giving that we receive.” This is so true.

My eight years as Pastor of St. Anne’s left a mark of love and belonging in my memory and heart. Yes, along with sorrow and pain, there was great joy and satisfaction. The good people gave me much love and affection, and I loved them - it was mutual. When I left, I grieved and cried, and experienced a terrible pain. However, as life moved on, I knew healing when I experienced the love from another community. Today I can only say “thank you” to the loving people of St. Anne’s. The day I packed up and drove away was a very sad day indeed.

Deo Gratias

Chapter 8

POPE FRANCIS

The time came when I realized I needed to move on from St. Anne’s, and see what else there was. At the time I had no idea I had such deep-rooted relationships with the parishioners. I thought that I could just walk away and be happy. I had never really grieved before. It was only looking back, that I realized I was grieving the loss of my closeness with my dearest friends.

I had a great pain in my heart that troubled me, which made it difficult to invest in another parish and group of people. Another factor bothering me, was to find out that after many years of promoting and working to build Vatican Council into parish life, the rest of the diocese had done little or nothing. They did change the language for the Mass and the Sacraments, and chose lay people to read the Scriptures, but that was about it. It almost felt as if I was stepping back in time when I saw that Vatican Council - second Pentecost as it was called - had not happened in the Parishes. It was a very upsetting observation to see that there was no new spirituality, or creative way of building the Kingdom of God here on Earth, and that the theology still spoke to saving souls rather than saving people.

When Pope Francis first became Pope, he found that there was tremendous pressure upon him to conform to what the Curia demanded, i.e. no change. Earlier, Pope Francis had identified clericalism as one of the great evils in the Church. He said the clergy had such a grip and control of the Church, it was impossible for the Church to grow into the 21st century, and meet the needs of the people. It became a Church of white privilege - not a universal Church.

I often say that I love the Church. Jesus said to love your neighbour. When I say love your neighbour, I am thinking of all the people I have met over the years - the people in Parry Sound, in Peterborough in the Parishes where I worked, and also the Protestants and atheists I met. I love you deeply.

It was the hierarchy of the day, the Priests, who conspired with the Roman authorities to have Jesus crucified. Jesus did not die on the cross for our sins. Jesus died on the cross because the authorities of the day conspired to get rid of Him, because they hated Him. When it comes to the hierarchy, on the one hand I will say that I love you, you are my brothers. However, I recognize that the vast majority are corrupt, power-hungry, controlling, white-privileged manipulators who refuse to join in the evolution toward a genuine Church of God in the 21st century.

I know that in many parts of the world Cardinals, Bishops and Priests are preaching and proclaiming celibacy as a gift from God, yet many of these men are sexually active. I know that many Cardinals groom young men, and then take them as their companions. I know that many Bishops are very sexually active, and we all know that many Priests have been sexually active with young children. Sexual assault and abuse has been one of the curses of the 20th and 21st centuries.

How can men like this, so corrupt in their morals, expect people to respect them and allow them to be our spiritual leaders? While I love them as a brother, I do not respect them, nor will I allow them to be any kind of authority in my life.

In the beginning of the reign of Pope Francis, it appeared that he was going to clean up the leadership of the Church. However, the opposition was too strong, and they had the power to resist. When Pope Francis had an opportunity to take a stance, he failed to do so. When he made his trip to Ireland, the Irish people expected the sexual abuse issue to be addressed. They were looking for hope and healing. What did they get? Silence. He said nothing about the issue, enjoyed the trip, and then went home.

Later when Pope Francis called for a synod in the Amazon, the people responded very positively and sent many great recommendations to Rome for the health and well-being of the Church. In the Amazon there is one Priest to every 100,000 people. In America there is one Priest to every 1,000 people. It was recommended that married men be allowed to be Priests, and that women be given a greater role in the Church - especially to be ordained as Deacons, and that Deacons eventually would be allowed to say Mass.

Everything was given a loud "no." It was a great opportunity for Pope Francis to show his caring for people. He failed. Yes, the Church in the Amazon continues with a shortage of Priests, and women are still treated as second-class citizens.

Pastoral Reflection

One thing Pope Francis was right about, was that clericalism is a great evil in the life of the Catholic Church. I know there have been, and still are, many good Priests and Bishops. When I was ordained, I stood on the shoulders of many of our Diocese Priests. I admired them, and learned a great deal from them. Many Clergy want to be in control, to be powerful, to give people God or deny people God, to be a good Churchman and be loyal to the Church - even if there is the unspoken word, don't worry about being loyal to God and the ways of Jesus. Allow people to put you on a pedestal because you are above the laity. By your ordination you are a person who has been transformed into something above and beyond the lay people. You are special, you belong to God, you are God's man, don't get your hands dirty, just do the minimal as far as your ministry is concerned. Enjoy the privileges that go with the Priesthood.

As far as the Church is concerned, I do agree that clericalism is one of the great evils that have evolved in the life of the Church. It perpetuates its life as new men are introduced to it. The power of clericalism has been able to block any progress that Pope Francis wanted in the LGBTQ community. One of the reasons he has been so frustrated, is that the vast majority of Cardinals, Bishops and Priests in various countries are homosexual, and have the power to push back against him. This is one more expression of corruption which has evolved among the clergy. It seems to be that if the lay people, or some other power, can eliminate clericalism, then the Church will continue. Or eventually it will not exist, at least not in its present form. In the end, people are not going to give up loving God, and knowing and loving Jesus.

Already I see a new Church being born, and small Christian communities are springing up. Christianity is meant to be the spiritual family of Jesus, in which He lives and brings justice and peace to the whole world. We as people of God have to find an honest way - find our voice - and have the courage to speak up, and speak out.

It is only when the people of God really use the voice of God, for the good of God, will things change for the better. Here in my Diocese, I know that I have been complacent. There is a saying that goes, "The only thing necessary for the triumph of evil, is for good men to do nothing." I feel that on this issue I am one of the men who has said nothing, and I will write about this in a future chapter.

Deo Gratias

Chapter 9

MY TINY HOUSE IN THE COUNTRY

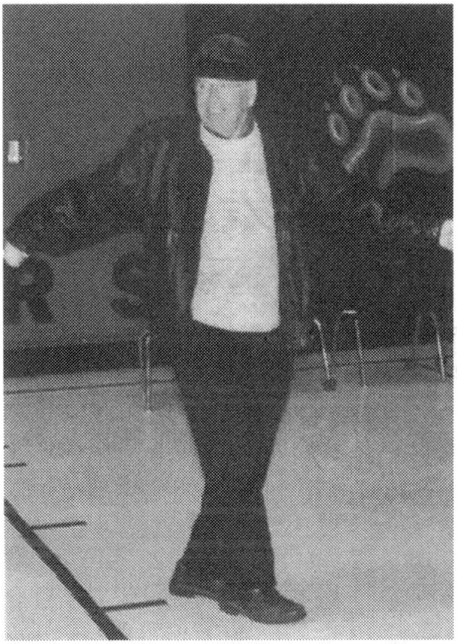

Father Leo Showing His Fancy Dance Steps

This period of my life was very tumultuous. I was appointed co-pastor of the parish in Port Hope, and was also part of the charismatic renewal. This was not a good arrangement. The Pastor was very traditional and controlling, and I was not allowed to do anything new. In the end it was either he had to resign, or I had to leave. I left.

At Christmas time I simply packed up my belongings, drove to my tiny house on the family farm and stayed there for the winter. My tiny house had everything I needed, even though it was very small. It gave me a chance to deal with my feelings - for healing, for wrestling with God, and above all - to get my spirituality more in line with the spirituality of the mystics. It was during this time that I realized the false image of God as a distant God, an authoritarian judge with the power to send people to hell, and I was able to begin to let go of this false God.

Reflecting on life itself and what I felt about God before the seminary, I was able to begin to see a God of intimacy, the God within and all around me, the God who loved me unconditionally and knew my name. This was traumatic for me. As a kid growing up, my own private spirituality was a God who was with me, a Jesus in my heart. I came to realize that the God I graduated from the seminary with, was not the God of my youth. The God of my youth was one I came to realize on my own, and it was a God of love and mercy - not a punitive God.

With this reflection I saw how the Church came to be like the God of the seminary. God as a judge who punished, who would send people to hell, and who had a set of requirements. Salvation was going to heaven and saving your own soul - not saving people. I saw how far this was removed from Jesus and the God of the gospels. I was faced with the reality of having to discover the God I knew as a youth.

There is a saying, "The longest journey you will make in your life is from your head to your heart." I learned this to be true, but I knew I had to discover the God in my heart if I was ever to go back to my ministry. I knew I could never go back and teach and preach the distant God - the judgmental and punitive God, the God of requirements. That in itself was a big turning point in my life. However, it was only like a seed that was sown, and would take years to germinate into my image of a completely different God.

I got a call from the Bishop, asking me to babysit an alcoholic pastor. I left my tiny home and returned to the city, and lived in the rectory. I found it was the "same old same old" – and just like living that song, "Give me that old time religion, it was good for our mothers, and it's good enough for me." I stayed in the parish for a few months, and then got another call from the Bishop to take over a parish where the pastor was on holiday. I guess he knew the pastor would not be returning, because in a few months I was assigned as Pastor to that parish.

Pastoral Reflection

Those months of living in my tiny house were the worst of times, but looking back it was also the best of times. It was a time of being aware of my inner world of turmoil and struggle, sorrow and pain. The big question facing me was, could I go back to the ministry seeing that the Church - not only in Peterborough but in many parts of Canada - had not really embraced Vatican II? It seemed that the Church was either dying or dead. Already people were starting to leave the Church in large numbers. As one author wrote, it was a hemorrhage as so many people were leaving the Church and turning elsewhere for spiritual nourishment. There was within me a restlessness, and a deep questioning of the future of a Church that seemed so resistant to Vatican II.

It was also a very lonely time because I felt alone. Living in my tiny house I had no one to really talk to, and to share with them my anger and my questioning. I knew that I could not call and talk openly and honestly with any other Priest. From the day of my ordination, I never felt comfortable belonging to the "Priest Club." They were more of the head while I lived out of intuition and imagination. It was like saying we were on two different wavelengths, and I knew we could not meet. I remember challenging a group of Priests I knew one evening, that I spoke for myself and that nobody agreed with me. The next day I heard one pastor say to another, "After what Father Leo said last night, I was not able to sleep." Needless to say, I really smiled at that and said, "Gotcha."

I remember the same thing happening at our Diocesan retreat, when we would have a clergy meeting. I would speak up, and tell them what I really thought regarding our belief system and pastoral practice. Twice I was reprimanded by an elderly pastor.

There seemed to be a distance between their thinking and my thinking. A couple of years after my ordination, I realized that the theology I had learned, for the most part was obsolete. At that point I decided to be a lifelong learner. This meant reading authors who wrote for today, going to seminars to hear speakers who were not always Catholics, but who were experts on scripture interpretation.

Looking back now, I can see how much I grew intellectually and spiritually. I think many of the Priests of the diocese finished at the seminary and then plateaued. I remember the Rector of the seminary telling my class, "You know all you need to know, so just go out there and tell them." A statement like that can show you how unprepared we were for the real world, when we had to minister to people who were struggling, trying to get ahead and survive, trying to find their way and raise a family, and then be told that they were sinners and that God could possibly send them to hell. What a terrible mindset to put before people!

I changed that, and told people over and over again, "God loves you, you are God's beloved, God loves you unconditionally and there is nothing you can ever do to separate yourself from God." I know from my own experience that I needed to be reaffirmed of God's love for me, so I could do the same for people and reaffirm them of their intrinsic goodness. I could tell them that they did not have to be afraid of God, as there is no judgment, no punishment, and no hell. I could tell them, "Go and live life fully and enjoy yourself - do this, and you will do what God wants you to do with your great gift of life."

Spending those moments in solitude and quiet, while lonely and painful, certainly were a blessing for me.

I faced the questions deep in my heart and soul. I did not always get an answer, but I learned to appreciate the language of God, which is silence. Silence taught me to trust God and to go forward.

At the Bishop's request I returned to active ministry, but I saw it from a whole new perspective. I saw the truth of my promise to God on the day of my first Mass, which was "put people first." I found out that to put people first, I had to follow the spirit. Just as Jesus acted out of a higher law - the law of love - so I acted in my ministry out of love. This meant that I had to override many of the rules and regulations of the Church. I was comfortable doing so, because I did it out of love, not anger.

Many times over the years I was reprimanded by various Bishops for breaking the rules. The ironic part was that by reprimanding me, I saw that I was right in what I was doing, so in a sense they were affirming my behavior. My guess is, the Bishops never saw this. What mattered to me most, was that for people struggling with their faith, or with situations that seemed impossible to resolve, we would find a way. It was experimentation and experience. I would move forward, deepen my sense of what it meant to be a Pastor, and also what it meant to put people first - which is exactly what Jesus did.

Deo Gratias

Chapter 10

BACK TO SCHOOL AND MY ILLNESS

The one gift that I became particularly interested in, was the healing ministry of Jesus and the promise of the Holy Spirit. As a Pastor, I established a healing Ministry in the city. This meant surrounding myself with volunteers and training them in active listening skills, training them to let go and pray under the power of the Holy Spirit. People came from far and wide - many struggling with living and with life. We became so busy that I resigned as Pastor. A family let us use half of their house, and I directed this house of prayer and healing for a couple of years. I had studied psychology - which enabled me to act as a psychotherapist - but I did not have a university degree.

I felt I was being urged to go to university and get a degree in counselling. I enrolled in the University of Ottawa and began the course. It was a fabulous time in my life, being a student and not having to be the leader. I enjoyed the relationships with my fellow students, and with the supervision I had to create counselling skills. I could have been a clinical psychologist. Things were going very nicely when at the end of January I had a heart attack. I dropped out of University and spent the next couple of months being tested by various doctors in a Toronto hospital. Eventually they found the problem, and the conclusion was that I had to have open heart surgery.

A friend of mine, whose uncle was a well-known heart surgeon in Ottawa, contacted him and he agreed to look after me. I went to the Ottawa hospital where the Toronto hospital had sent all my files, and the doctor knew exactly what had to be done. I remember the night before the surgery he came to see me and asked me if I had any questions. I replied, "I have one, am I going to die tomorrow?" He answered, "Probably not," and I did not. The operation went fine, and yet it was the consequences of the surgery that almost did me in.

I had always been proud of the strength of my body. Being raised on a farm, I had no need to go to a gym as there was always enough hard work on the farm. After the operation I was extremely weak, and was told that I could no longer be involved in heavy physical activity such as sports. When I came home from Ottawa, I stayed in one of our Parish rectories, and yet it was not a freebee. I had to pay room and board, and did not have a job. I still had part of a semester to complete, in order to get my degree. I connected with a clinical psychologist who journeyed with me, and brought me to the point where I could get my M.A.

That was the worst time in my life. I was so weak, I knew my life had changed forever. Not only did I lose my physical strength, I lost connection with friends with whom I had played squash. Plus, I still did not have a paying job. I experienced depression and hopelessness for the future. It looked very bleak.

I decided to accept an appointment to a parish, and began a counselling ministry by myself. The parish provided me with room and board, a secretary, and a counselling facility. Initially I wondered if anyone would show up for counselling. By now I had learned how to mix psychological skills with the gift of the Holy Spirit. The grapevine must have worked in my favor, because soon I was working full-time in the counselling and healing ministries. I really saw the love that God showered upon people as they experienced healing, transformation, and the freedom to live a full life.

The one difference with my ministry was that it was primarily developed to help the poor. I would never get rich with my ministry, unlike other psychotherapists, who charged from $75 - $100 per hour. I did not charge those rates. In my first session, a client asked how much he owed me, and I said nothing at all, I don't charge. However, if you want to make a donation, that would be fine. Many clients paid $10 - $20 per session. As I look back on the ten years of my counselling ministry, I realized how blessed those days were. As I worked, I saw people experiencing healing, growth, and transformation.

Pastoral Reflection

After ten years as a Minister in the Healing Ministry, combining psychology with spirituality in a God acting, God loving, and God healing modality, one of the things I gained was a greater awareness and belief that Jesus would always be with me. Jesus constantly showed up, when I turned to faith imagery to touch the minds and hearts of people. When I saw things happening and people living as they did, I trusted that it was God acting in their lives. I saw a God who simply did not look upon people suffering.

God was right at the center of people's suffering, whether it was anxiety, oppression, or another issue a person was dealing with. I saw that God suffered when people suffered, and this helped to change my image of God. It became very personal for me, during the difficult times of my life. I knew that God was suffering with me in my suffering. Today as I still journey with people who are suffering, I see the presence of a loving God, and how that love is released from my heart to their heart. There is a very strong connection, and I am continually reminded that God is with me, and loving me every moment of my life. It is a strong reminder that God is with us, and is feeling the pain of all victims of oppression, war, poverty and homelessness - in other words the pain of the world. I see that God is not playing it safe by being a distant God. I hold to the transcendence of God, and also to the eminence of God.

To me incarnation is very real. Not only the incarnation of Jesus, but the incarnation of myself and all the people of the world, all living creatures, all animals, and Mother Earth herself. I have come to realize, that all of creation experiences pain. I can see that God is incarnated not only in people, but in all of creation.

Looking back and reflecting on the ten years of practicing psychotherapy, it is with a sense of satisfaction, and with the feeling that I was really doing God's work. We know that Jesus did God's work by His healing of the sick and troubled. We know that Jesus said we would receive the Holy Spirit and be able to do His work, and even more. I would never say what I did was greater than what Jesus did by reintroducing the Healing Ministry into the Peterborough Church, and yet through this healing ministry many people experienced the presence, the love, and the healing power of Jesus. I am sure it helped people to develop a stronger belief in the reality of God and Jesus in their life.

At the end of ten years I was thinking of retirement, and I wanted to retire as a Pastor. I knew I had four years to go before reaching the age of seventy, at which point I would retire. A Parish came open. I had made it known to the Bishop that I was ready and able to Pastor again. Thank God he appointed me as a Pastor, and I was able to end my career as I had wanted, as a Parish Pastor for four more years, after which time I retired.

Deo Gratias

Chapter 11

MY LAST PARISH

Fr. Leo with his guitar and his band

I was assigned to St. Alphonsus as Pastor, a parish with truly wonderful people. I knew that I had four years left in Parish ministry, and then I was going to retire. When I approached the Bishop after my four years and told him I wanted to retire, he said “No.” I am a very stubborn man. I went back a second time and received the answer “No.” I went back a third time and received a “Yes.”

I loved being a Pastor and very much enjoyed walking with people along the highway of life. However, I felt that 70 years old was the right time to retire. It also meant I could move on in pastoral ministry without having to worry about administration. It felt good to remove that monkey from my back. There were baptisms, weddings, planning of liturgies, preaching, and bringing forward the emerging faith story, that blended Catholic faith with new scientific discoveries.

I did a great deal of reading of various authors, and in them I saw a whole new interpretation of the meaning of the word "God," and a much better teaching and understanding of the teachings of Jesus. I saw that parish life could be more actively involved in the world. It was important to see that the word salvation no longer meant being a good person for a lifetime, dying in a state of grace, and zooming up to heaven.

Science showed that it was not a three-tier universe, rather that all was one. One holistic organism, without any up or down. Elevator theology was dead. Instead of meaning a successful journey up to heaven, the word "salvation" meant the saving of people right here and right now. Saving of people from injustice, hunger, starvation, oppression and from being called sinners, instead of being called God's beloved. The new cosmology changed it all, as well as the understanding of biology and evolution. The old theology was built on a three-tier universe, and since it no longer existed it would be evolution now and ongoing, until the end of time.

The realization that we as human beings, are evolving slowly but surely, means that the next generation will build on what we have become, and this will go on until the end of time. I found it very exciting to bring the emerging new faith story to the people of God. I found for myself as well, that my spiritual life took a great leap forward as I wrestled with, read about and experienced the emerging new faith story. It is so unfortunate that the Church with its preaching and teaching, is still stuck in the previous century and the three-tier universe.

During this time there are many movements that are starting to surface in our Church and in the world. There is a sense that we are a global village, even though we are separated on a map from many countries. We are one, one God, one people - and creation is the Body of God. In the emerging new faith story God is both transcendent and eminent.

Incarnation means the son of God became human in the person of Jesus. The truth of the Incarnation helps us to see not only that Jesus was God become human, but it also shows that we are God become human. I think this is one of our crowning glories. But the majority of people do not really believe it (at least that is the way I see it).

My last four years as a Pastor were very satisfying years. The number of people attending Mass grew. I cancelled the Parish Council, because the Priest before me told me that they were too resistant to progress. I felt that after four years the next Pastor could have an elected Parish Council.

Another thing I became aware of was feminism. We know that for many years, women have been simply regarded as second-class citizens, and denied equality. Pope Francis made it clear that women were not to be ordained to the Priesthood. It seems that he has a blind spot when it comes to women. For centuries Church authorities have denied women the right to ordination, claiming that Jesus only wanted men. That is a wrong reading of the gospels. Women journeyed with Jesus, and supported Him when He was dying on the cross. The choosing of only men is a means to dominate and control. Modern-day women are seeing the error in this kind of thinking.

The Anglican Church has female Priests, the United Church has female ministers, and many Christian religions have female leaders and pastors. It seems that only the Catholic Church hangs on to an old tradition, based on a false interpretation of Scripture. To me, the Church hierarchy will not see a good thing, even when clearly shown. That is power and control, even at the great loss of people. Through the Church, they hang onto their comfortable lifestyle, which demands power and control. I hope that someday there will be a hierarchy who will wake up and see the harm they are doing to the body of Christ, and how they are ruling over a Church that is failing the people. Hopefully one day, women will be honored with the right to ordination if they ask for it.

As I look back on these four years, it is with a sense of finality that we are moving forward in the right direction. There are so many different writers, well informed and competent, who are bringing forward the emerging new story of faith and science. It is exciting to see that science needed faith, and that God and religion needed science.

For a long time the Church has been suspicious of science. I saw this suspicion by the reluctance of Church authorities to become informed and educated, or to see the blending of faith and science as good news, and a beautiful new story. I remember helping set up the St. Vincent de Paul Society in the parish. The food banks were primarily downtown, and it was a long walk for the poor to go there for food. A group of parish people came up with the idea of establishing a food bank in the parish, and a meeting room was needed. I found a small room that was unused, and we agreed to use it for storing food. I said there would only be one rule, "That anyone who comes here will get as much food as they want, and it is not to be measured out in any way." The people agreed and business began. We had large numbers of people from the west end come to our food bank. They received not only food for the body but also for the soul, because people met them with hospitality and a warm welcome. They did not have to justify their needs, and we got to know their names. This was one of the really good things that we established in my last four years.

Another thing I really enjoyed was playing my guitar at Mass. Since I could not play sports anymore, I decided to take up learning the guitar. I bought a guitar, got a sheet of paper with chords on it and practiced for an hour each day. Soon I was able to make music. I formed a small band and we were able to go out and entertain. I played the lead guitar and even sang. However, one of my singers realized I could not carry a tune, so she would turn off my microphone so nobody could hear my singing. I thought this was a great example of healthy relationships, when she knew I would not be offended by living the truth. I cannot sing! I have always loved music, love to laugh, and enjoy making other people laugh.

I learned a supply of jokes, and when we were entertaining people I would be a comedian. It was so exciting to hear and see the people laughing at my dumb jokes. In the summertime I gave the Parish organist the summer off. I asked a person to come and sing at the Sunday Mass, and I played guitar. This I really enjoyed. After I left the Parish, I gave my guitars away. Now twenty years later, I have obtained another guitar and I am learning to play once again. However, my fingers are twenty years older. They are stiff, and even though I remember the chords, my fingers need a lot of practice before I can really play. I love music. I bought Alexa so that I can choose my own music to listen to for enjoyment. It is too bad that I am so old, because you will not be able to invite me to offer music ministry at your family gatherings! I know that if you did, and I played my guitar and sang, I can promise you I would spoil your party! When I get to heaven, I am going to ask St. Peter to give me a singing voice, and then I will come back to Earth and entertain everyone.

Deo Gratias

Chapter 12

MORALITY

Father Leo & Ginger

This story is about sex and a single person, sex and married couples, and sex and same-sex couples. It is hard to know where to begin with this particular part of my life. I attended public elementary and secondary schools, and even though we were very much aware of sex we never really talked about it. The teachers never talked about it, because at that time it was not part of the curriculum. Over the years, I have run into many Catholics who attended Catholic schools and were taught about sex. One thing they were taught, was that it was a "no-no" to have sex of any kind until after marriage. If they did it was a serious sin, and if they did not repent and go to confession, when they died they were sure to go to hell. This kind of teaching in the Catholic schools and from the local Pastor, was more than enough to give people a very negative attitude toward the enjoyment of sex, and also a feeling of guilt.

I attended a Catholic secondary school for Grade 13 and there was a lot of talk about sex. It was an all-boys school and we were repeatedly told not to do "it," whatever the hell "it" was. Again coming from a public school, what I was taught seemed kind of crazy to me.

For example, one Priest said if a boy went to the bathroom to have a leak, and when through urinating shook it more than three times it was a venal sin, and if he shook it more than five times it was mortal sin. Since it was an all-boys school, there was a lot of condemnation of masturbation and impure thoughts. After ordination, I discovered that these views trapped many people in fear and guilt.

There were married people who were taught very clearly that it was mortal sin to practice artificial birth control. I met many people who quit the Church because of that teaching. A papal cyclical in 1967 made it very clear that artificial birth control was sinful. The Pope put together a commission to study the issue of artificial birth control, and the majority of the members came to the conclusion that it was time to drop the restriction on this. However, the Pope of the day was too timid to follow the recommendations of the committee, and he reasserted that Catholic couples must not practice artificial birth control.

The Canadian Bishops met in Winnipeg, and they came up with the resolution called "responsible parenthood." This basically meant that couples were to follow their conscience. There was a strong teaching against fornication, artificial birth control, masturbation, adultery and same-sex relationships. I refer to all of these as "pelvic morality." It seems that the Church is obsessed with pelvic morality, and Catholic people are living with much guilt around sex.

For many years people were not aware of homosexuality, and as a result it was not included in the early Church. Recently, as the topic of same-sex relationships became well-known, the Church once again showed its hand by saying that homosexuality was being "intrinsically disordered" or "objectively disordered." When Pope Francis first became Pope and was asked about the question of homosexuality, he refused to be a judge. He also came out recently with another statement, saying that Priests were not to officiate at same sex marriages. This is what I call the "Vatican two-step." One step forward, and one step back.

I know the LGBTQ community has suffered a great deal at the hands of this kind of thinking and morality. It seems to me that it is time for the Church to get out of the public morality business, and let people follow their conscience to build relationships that are loving and life-giving. Certainly, many same sex relationships are truly loving and life-giving.

Pastoral Reflection

Our Church authorities have a lot to learn about sex in general, the Canadian Catholic community, and members of the LGBTQ community. When we read the gospels, we find that Jesus said very little about sex. He said a great deal about compassion, about understanding people, about not judging people, and affirming all people of their intrinsic goodness. It is obvious today that young Catholic couples are not paying any attention to the official Church, which continues to teach that artificial birth control is sinful. Most Catholic couples have two children. This shows the mindset of young Catholic couples.

When we consider the LGBTQ community, we can see how the official Church has really screwed this up. Scientists report that at least 1,500 different species have homosexual members. This shows that homosexuality is very normal and natural. The claim that homosexual is intrinsically disordered, or an objective disorder, shows a lack of knowledge and a lack of understanding on human sexuality. We know that members of the LGBTQ community have been discriminated against for a long time by the official Church. We also know that many Priests and Bishops are not only gay, but are in relationships and sexually active. It seems that the clergy who are always speaking out against homosexuality, are the same ones trying to cover up their own gay sexual orientation. They need to be totally ignored.

I attended a gay/straight alliance at a high school for several years. One year the issue of same-sex marriage came up in conversation, when a man with some theological training trotted out the old saying that the purpose of marriage was to beget children and control concupiscence.

That old chestnut needs to be laid to rest forever - this is the 21st century! One of the teachers asked me what my attitude was towards same-sex marriage. My response was very clear, "Two people love each other, God is love, and therefore their relationship is Godly. And of course, I would be glad to officiate at their wedding." I would never discriminate against someone whose sexual orientation was different than mine. I know many same-sex couples, some married and some not, but they are living love in a very tender and kind way. In my humble opinion same-sex couples deserve the same kind of pastoral care as everyone else.

The Church needs to appoint competent, well-educated and well-balanced people who can separate fact from fiction, and devise a spirituality around sexuality. Remember when Jesus invited people, He did not exclude anyone - all were included and all were welcome! We, the Church of the 21st century, are obliged to be true to Jesus and His vision and teachings. A Church that excludes or discriminates is not the Church of Jesus. Our pastoral ministry must follow the example of Jesus, as anything less is clearly a sin.

I believe the LGBTQ community have been excluded for too long. I also believe we need to open our eyes and embrace them, welcome them as our equals, and offer them the same pastoral care that we offer all people.

Deo Gratias

Chapter 13

CANON LAW

One of the courses I took in the seminary was canon law, which is the laws of the Church written down by authorities in the Church. I never had the sense that it was God speaking, or God's will for the people. The canon law that I studied for four years was published in 1918, and was considered very up-to-date. It may have been up-to-date in 1918, but it was still legalism at its worse. When you read the gospels you find that Jesus challenged legalism, because he saw it as restricting, and enslaved the people. It also demanded a high degree of obedience to the law, and breaking the law carried serious consequences in the community. Jesus wanted people to understand that he came to liberate them from blind obedience. He often made reference to the time they were slaves in Egypt, and how God had liberated them and brought them to the Promised Land, a land of milk and honey. There are many examples in the gospel that show how Jesus, out of love for the people, rose above the law and acted. For example, it was forbidden that we heal on the Sabbath, but moved by compassion, Jesus healed those who needed healing.

Jesus showed us an example of living love and living compassion. Doing justice, it may seem strange that I experienced the Catholic Church with legalism, but that was what I found very soon after ordination.

Of course, we know that legalism on one hand empowered the clergy, and on the other disempowered lay people. With canon law, clergy were able to control and dominate lay people, as they had the power. It was believed that canon law gave clergy the authority to give God, or refuse to give God, to people. For example, clergy telling people they would not baptize their baby, officiate at their wedding, or offer them communion. Naturally this kind of power made it a very unbalanced relationship between the clergy and the people. Clergy had the power to control and oppress the people. People in the parish knew they had been disempowered by the force of canon law, which they had no chance to study. They had to take someone else's word for it. The same people had been taught not to think for themselves and not to follow their own conscience, but rather to seek permission from the Pastor. Thus they were very vulnerable to power and control over their lives.

I certainly saw this time and again when I was growing up in my parish. I often wondered why adults were so dependent on the Pastor for permission to live their own way. As a Priest I encouraged people to think critically, to think for themselves, and to apply their own moral principles to any decision they had to make, and to trust that they would make the right decision. I wanted them to understand that they did not have to consult the local Pastor, if they wanted to be free and life their life as mature adults.

Pastoral Reflection

It was not long after ordination, when I came to realize the legalism of the Institution, the power in the hands of the Pastor, the disempowerment of the people of the parish, and how they were at the mercy of the goodwill of the Pastor. I remember one time when we had a very wet summer, my mother would go to the Pastor and ask if it would be all right to harvest on Sunday. The Pastor was not a country boy, but he always gave permission for my father and brothers to harvest on Sunday. I do believe that farmers have now outgrown that unhealthy dependency.

First, I will mention the Principle of Double Effect which is so important for people when they are on the horns of a dilemma, particularly in the fields of healthcare or surgery. The same situation can occur when a woman is pregnant and ready to give birth, and suddenly there are complications to both the baby and mother. Here the Principle of Double Effect is extremely important for the parents to know, if they choose a course of action that may have a negative result to either the mother or the baby. Again, the mother does not need to consult with the Pastor, in order to get moral guidance. She knows the Principle of Double Effect, and is able to make a decision knowing there is no guilt, or need to regret the decision.

The second principle I learned from a Priest from Buffalo, was the principle Epekia. This has been one of the most important moral principles that I was taught in the seminary. Epekia means that when faced with a moral dilemma, there are several conditions to be met in order to act in an ethical manner. The first is to know the total situation, to research it and be familiar with any moral principles that apply to the situation, to pray for guidance, and to make sure that the action taken is done from love, compassion and justice. Spaces where I used Epekia most frequently were at funerals, where people did not want to use the Church, but wanted the funeral Mass in the funeral home Chapel. For some unknown reason, to celebrate a funeral Mass in a funeral home is forbidden. Yet on some occasions it is the preferred location for the family. I have celebrated a funeral Mass in the funeral home Chapel many times, and several times I was reported to the Bishop of the day. Of course, this is going to result in an invitation to visit the Bishop and be reprimanded! However, I never apologized for it, because I knew in my heart that I did the right thing, and I will not apologize for doing the right thing. Again, Jesus has shown me the way.

The third moral principle I learned from the dogmatic Priest/ Professor from Buffalo, was the principle to minister to people entering a second marriage without an annulment.

The rule was that if a Catholic was going to enter into a second marriage and his/her future partner had been married before, they would have to get a declaration to nullify their first marriage from the Church. First there was an interrogation by the Marriage Tribunal, and then it may be referred to the Vatican for a final decision on the validity of the first marriage. Many people certainly felt that this was an invasion of privacy, as he/she was in love and simply wanted to get married, live together and get on with life.

I remember the first couple who came to me in this situation. When I was stationed at Sacred Heart Parish in 1964, a young woman rang the doorbell and asked to see me. I welcomed her into the office. We chatted and then I asked what I could do for her. She told me that she simply wanted to be married, but there was a problem. Her future husband was married before, and when she had gone to see another Priest, her uncle, he told her that because of the Catholic Church law he could do nothing for her unless he got an annulment. She continued on to say that her boyfriend was a Protestant, and he would not have anything to do with getting an annulment.

I remembered the day at the seminary when the professor taught the moral principle and the Internal Form to officiate at a valid marriage, when one partner had not sought or obtained an annulment. This was 1964, and deliberately breaking the law of the Church at that time was very risky. However, I remembered that when faced with a difficult situation, Jesus was moved by compassion, and was then able to minister to the people. First of all I talked to her about confidentiality, and if we could agree to keep things quiet between us I could possibly help her. She promised that her lips were sealed. I explained to her the process of the Internal Form, which was much like confession. It was very much a part of the Church's teaching - not my own - and we could go ahead and perform the marriage under those conditions. I suggested she obtain a marriage license and bring it to me, and then we would set a wedding date using the principle of the Internal Form.

A week later on a Saturday morning the young couple arrived at the rectory, and we had a ceremony of mutual consent and acknowledgement of consent under the authority of the Church. On Sunday morning after Mass, I went to the nearby coffee shop and there were several parishioners sitting at a table having coffee. One of the men said to me, "I hear you had a wedding on Saturday." For the next two weeks I did not answer the phone, as I fully expected the Peterborough grapevine to take it to Head Office, and the mud would hit the fan. It did not happen.

I wrote earlier, that during my first Mass at St. Paul's Church in Norwood, I heard a voice within me that said, "Fr. Leo, I want you to put people first." I soon found out that the pastoral ministry of putting people first was the most important attitude to bring to my ministry. I always felt that I was to be a channel of grace, to liberate people from the restraints of the past, to set them free from legalism, lack of knowledge and the secrets of the Church. Acting in this way, I have been able to faithfully serve many people.

I know that many people have been very angry at some of the ways I act in favor of people. However, I make no apologies for putting people first, and rising above legalism. There are many different ways in which life unfolds. Life has its own agenda, and very often it does bring hardships into people's lives such as mental illness, poverty, physical illness, grieving over the death of a loved one, on so on. I hope and pray to God, that when I come to the end of my road of life, I may possibly hear the words, "Well done, faithful servant." Faithful servant, yes indeed! My vocation and ministry have been to serve the people of God - without any discrimination, judgment or criticism - as a servant, not as a superior. I now see how giving up blind obedience was liberating for me.

Deo Gratias

Chapter 14

THE WORD SALVATION

I reflect on the idea expressed by using the word “salvation.” In the Old Testament, the Israelite people believed salvation was in their liberation from Egypt, added to their arrival at the Promised Land. To them, that was salvation, because they were no longer slaves but free people. However, the Romans came and the people were once again oppressed, and no longer free in their own land. The religious leaders seemed to flourish if they collaborated with the Romans, and were allowed a certain measure of self determination. Unfortunately, the people suffered from their own leaders and the Roman taxation system. Once again, they were in need of liberation and salvation. When Jesus showed up on the scene, they wondered if he was going to be the Messiah. Would he raise an army and drive the oppressing Romans out of their land? And yet Jesus disappointed them. He told them that His Kingdom was not of this world - meaning a Kingdom not of oppression - but a Kingdom of love, justice and peace. Jesus had many conflicts with the religious leaders of the day. As a matter of fact, He called them hypocrites because they laid heavy burdens on the people, and did not lift a finger to alleviate their suffering. Naturally the religious leaders came to hate Jesus, and plotted his untimely death.

After Pentecost and the coming of the Holy Spirit, slowly but surely the Christian communities came into being and grew very quickly.

It was in Corinth that they were called Christians for the first time. For 300 years the Christian communities grew in the Middle East. During this time, there was no overarching authority to rule over all the Christian communities. They were led and inspired by the Holy Spirit individually, to carry on the work of God. However, in the 4th century, Roman Emperor Constantine wanted to unify the people of the Roman Empire, and he looked to a religion that would help him do that. He chose Christianity.

He declared that Christianity would be the religion of the Empire, and that the leaders of Christianity - the people we call Bishops today - would be closely aligned with the ruling authorities. The Emperor sat in the main chair in the governing room. On his right hand sat the second in command, and on his left side sat a Bishop. There is an old Protestant hymn that sums this up as, "They exchanged the cross for the crown." The Bishops had temporal power in the Roman Empire, and I suppose in some ways this was the beginning of the compromise made by Christians. Jesus had made it very clear that His kingdom was not of this world, and yet with Constantine the leaders compromised themselves. Over the centuries this arrangement has dearly cost Christianity.

In the 4th century St. Augustine, a great theologian, appeared on the scene. He came to Christianity as a result of his mother's prayers. There is no doubt he was a very intelligent man. He created a theology which has played out in the Christian Church ever since. He considered the story of the Garden of Eden, and Adam and Eve. There are many lessons to be learned from the story of Adam and Eve, but St. Augustine proposed that disobedience in the garden was a terrible sin, and thus they were cast out of the garden. By sinning they had broken their relationship with God, and all people for all time were included in that broken relationship. He taught that original sin was carried by every baby when they were born, and that baby had to be baptized for salvation. Today we realize that this theology is wrong, and causes people anguish when their baby dies without being baptized.

St. Augustine invented limbo, and please notice that I say "invented" limbo. In the 11th century Bishop Anslem dug a deeper hole as he taught the idea of atonement. The culture at the time was feudal, which meant that when a subject acted against the Lord of the Manor, they must make retribution in order to restore his/her relationship with the Lord of the Manor. Bishop Anslem reasoned that it was the same with God. In his opinion, the people had broken their relationship with God and they needed to atone for their sins in order to win back God's friendship. This notion of atonement is one of the worst theological theories ever foisted upon believers. Original sin was bad enough, but the theory of atonement added to people's burdens. Bishop Anslem went on to say that the coming of Jesus into the world was to atone for the sins of humankind, and that he did this by dying on the cross, shedding his blood for the sins of the world. Ever since then, Christians have gathered on Good Friday to honor this false belief.

The idea of atonement, reconciliation and the death of Jesus for the sins of the world, is all included in the Eucharistic prayer of our Mass. As many people hear the Eucharistic prayer on Sunday morning, I often wonder if they hear the words, or they have heard it so often they don't even think about it. If that is the case, and it simply passes over their heads without acknowledging the words, are they praying about what they have heard and felt? It is important for us to realize that the Church is still strongly rooted in the notion of original sin, and the absolute need for baptism as salvation. The Church is still strongly rooted in the notion of atonement, and this comes up in the prayers of the Mass, and most of the others read from prayer books that have been written for Catholics. In my humble opinion, the theory of atonement is false and needs to be trashed. If we were to have a better interpretation of scripture, we would see that the notion of original sin and atonement are simply the ideas of two theologians who made an error. We need new Eucharistic prayers that emphasize not sin, but God's presence, God's actions and God's unconditional love for all creation - including humans and all living beings.

Pastoral Reflection

As I reflect on the background of our religion, both original sin and atonement, I realize just how far we have drifted from the teachings of Jesus. I am not surprised that we have taken the word "salvation" and entirely misinterpreted it. Salvation has meant that if you lived a good life – of course obedient to the voice of the Church - you died in a state of grace and then took an elevator up to heaven where God waited for you. It was a common belief before Vatican II that when you died, you appeared before God to be judged. And it was commonly believed that God was the judge of the living and dead, and could punish people and send them to purgatory or hell. Do we really believe that God has written everything we have done wrong in a Book of Life, and that when we appear on the scene God has our history and will judge us to be welcome in heaven, or will we need to clean up our act in purgatory, or go to hell forever? This is the image of God that has been handed down to believers for many centuries, and it is totally wrong.

Jesus was always telling people that they had to change their minds about God. Psychologists tell us that the most difficult thing a human being can do is change his/her mind. When people believe in hell for 50, 60, or 70 years, they think they are right, and do not want to hear anything different. When they do hear something different, a new fresh idea, they may become angry, and even violent.

But the truth of the matter is, God is both transcendent and eminent. The best description for God that I have seen, comes from an article written by Rabbi Shapiro that says, "God is the source and the substance of all that is." When we say that God is eminent we mean that God is right here, living in our hearts and in our midst. We believe that our bodies are the temple of the Holy Spirit, and that the spirit of the living God lives within us. The Incarnation tells us that God became human not just in Jesus, but in every human being born into this world. God knows us and calls us by name, and carries us in the palm of His hand.

With this story, we realize that God loves each and every one of us unconditionally, and we do not fear God's judgment. The emerging new faith story that I am using for my reference and reflection, gives me an image of a God dwelling in my heart, and loving me unconditionally. If you are ready to take His word seriously, you can see that God is not a judge, and is not punitive. Basically, the only thing God can do is to love us unconditionally, no matter how good we are, or how bad we are. To God it makes no difference. I want to take this idea just a little further.

The traditional story is that heaven comes after life, on Planet Earth. As I have said, since heaven is where God is, and God is here living in our hearts, then heaven is right here - right now. You and I are in heaven at this very moment, and will be forever. There is nothing to fear from God. This also helps us to arrive at the conclusion that since nothing can separate us from God, there is no purgatory, hell, or limbo. We believe that we live in God, now and forever. This is the good news that Jesus brought to the people of God. Unfortunately, down through the centuries, because of the teachings of people like St. Augustine and Bishop Anselm, the teachings of the Church went astray. Now in the 21st century we are able to see this, and to create a new faith story that is filled with love and hope, and that focuses on joy, not fear. A faith story that sets us free to love ourselves. We are not sinners - we are God's beloved - and our challenge is to love God, all people, all of creation, and to bring about the kingdom of God here on Earth.

We have a mission from God, and that is to do God's work. We must know very clearly what God's work is, and to be busy with it. Otherwise, we will fail our God, and fail our mission for being born here on Earth for such a short time. In conclusion, I want to stress that the word salvation as used in scripture (the New Testament) does not mean you will go to heaven when you die. No - it has everything to do with this life on Earth. We experience salvation by experiencing God, and God's unconditional love for us, and that gives us the freedom to live human life fully.

We see salvation as having to do with social justice, and unconditional love for all that is. Salvation is the coming of the Kingdom of God into the hearts of people. The people who are oppressed, hungry, poor, depressed or hopeless; wealthy people who are enslaved to riches; political leaders who are self-serving; and in particular, religious leaders who need to be better educated in the ways of God. Also, Seminary education needs to be reformed.

To become a competent Pastor, a person must be a life-long student in order to be informed on evolution, the sciences, and up-to-date spiritualities that give us a better explanation of the evolving new faith story. It seems to me, that unless the Pastors of our Churches are competent and relevant, the people in the pews will remain immature and ill-equipped to do the work of God. This is the main reason why we are here on Earth, and have been gifted with faith in a loving God. The word salvation within the Christian community no longer means dying in a state of grace, and going up to heaven. The word salvation for us means investing our energy, time and talent to do God's work, which is to bring about the Kingdom of God on Earth in the hearts of people. This is the reason for being born into this world.

Deo Gratias

Chapter 15

TRANSFORMATION OF MY PRAYER LIFE

I grew up on a farm. My family went to Mass on Sundays, and my father had promised his mother that he would always lead his family in prayer with the rosary every evening, which he did. As kids we were taught to say morning and evening prayers. We memorized them, got down on our knees, and faithfully said our prayers every day. However, there was some kind of yearning in my soul, a yearning for something more. I remember a group of tall pine trees standing on our farm, and as a ten-year old child, found myself attracted to these tall trees and frequently visited them. In the middle of the tall pine trees I built a little shelter, and this became my Chapel. There was a small stream winding its way past my Chapel, the chipmunks would come to play, and the birds would sing. I heard whispers in the tall pines, and there was silence. It was there that I learned the language of God, the language of silence, and the beauty of stillness and quiet. As I read scripture passages, the one that stood out to me was, "Be still and know that I am God." I found the meaning of being still and silent before God. I did not know the name of this experience at the time, but later I learned it was called "meditation."

It was in the midst of the tall pines that I met God, and it was in the midst of the tall pines that my soul was nourished. I discovered a God of unconditional love and compassion - so unlike the God I had met in the Baltimore catechism.

In nature, I met a God who was close to me and loved me unconditionally. The God of the catechism was a distant God who would judge and condemn. One summer I returned home and discovered that the tall pines were gone. I asked my brother Charlie what had happened, and he told me that a house builder had bought them. He had looked at the trees and saw lumber, and my brother had looked at the trees and saw money. I was sad to see my Chapel gone.

My form of prayer life took another big change when I entered the seminary. We had mediation every morning, but it was not even a prayer. We had a book from which we read a passage, and afterwards had to answer four or five questions. This went on for seven years, and I forgot how to sit in silence with God. Even after ordination, we were to say the official prayers of the Church every day. I did not find prayer time in the seminary, or reading the prayers of the Church, as nourishing for my soul.

After a great deal of searching, I dropped them all and again took up meditation. That has been my model of prayer for the last fifty years. Twice a day, morning and evening, I pause, go to a quiet space and be mindful of the words I have known for so long, "Be still and know that I am God."

I sit in silence, and listen to the God within me. The God who knows me and calls me by name, the God who loves me unconditionally, the God dwelling in my heart and all around me, and the God of love and intimacy whom I need not fear. It is a God with no requirements - not even to be good - since God loves me unconditionally, and I believe that neither life nor death, nor anything in between, can separate us from the love of God. I believe that scripture has set me free. I no longer fear God, and our relationship is one of unconditional love with total acceptance.

Pastoral Reflection

Upon reflecting on my own spirituality and the spirituality of parishioners, it seemed that saying prayers was not really prayer at all. The language of God is silence, and if we are to pray with God we have to learn God's language. Fifty years ago I was introduced to Father Thomas Keating, the Priest who promoted centering prayer as a form of meditation. This model of prayer became my model of prayer, that I have faithfully followed twice a day. I also discovered that many parishioners found it difficult to pray.

Before Vatican Council II, many were faithful to memorize prayers twice a day, but it was not particularly a growth experience. Some told me that they did not pray anymore, because it was meaningless to them. Also, memorized prayers led them to have certain expectations of God. Many times they prayed asking for something, and were disappointed when God did not seem to answer their prayers. So then they were angry toward God, whom they felt had failed them in their hour of need.

After taking up the practice of Father Thomas Keating's centering prayer, and drawing on my own experience, I made the decision to offer classes on meditation and centering prayer. I found that those classes met the needs of many people. When I worked for the School Board I would advertise a class on centering prayer, and in a few days it would have a full registration. Many were teachers wishing to enrich and strengthen their spirituality. They were ready to turn to a new form of prayer, sitting in silence, and learning the language of God in stillness, while experiencing God's dwelling presence within their heart.

We believe that our bodies are temples of the Holy Spirit. Many who attended those classes have continued to this day with this form of prayer. Their spirituality has been transformed, and brought awareness to them regarding their relationship with God. I saw in the parish the same hunger and thirst for a more intimate relationship with the Divine, and parishioners were very open and receptive to attending classes on centering prayer and meditation.

In so doing, their relationship with God became transformed and growth-oriented, when they realized the blessing of sitting in silence and not bombarding God with words.

In recent years I have continued to define my own spirituality, which is deeply rooted in centering prayer. Often in the evenings the first thought that strikes me is, "I am too tired." I know that this is a distraction to take me away from spending 20 minutes in meditation. It seems to me that if there are going to be Christians in the future, they will have to do what Jesus did, and make prayer a priority in their life. At the present time it seems to me that too many people are trying to get along on their own. They either leave the Christian life, or drop out all together. Needless to say, this will not help to build the Kingdom of God here on Earth.

Part of the problem is that Christians have been taught to be good in order to get to heaven, but that is not it. Heaven is a gift from God, and we never have to worry or work to experience heaven. However, Jesus made it clear in his teachings that we are here to do God's work, and God's work is about creating the Kingdom of God on Earth. This seems to be one of the most difficult teachings of Jesus to get across to people. This is especially true of clergy, who continue to teach and preach that being good is the object of one's spiritual life in order to escape hell, and get a good judgment call into heaven. This is wrong. Our tasks are to do God's work, and Jesus showed us that God's work is to bring about the Kingdom of God on Earth. When this happens, it will be a world of justice, peace, friendship, and kindness - in short, a world where everyone will have enough. It will be a completely New World Order.

The early Christians thought Jesus would return very soon, but now we realize that it may be several million years before God's plan has been accomplished. Having said that, already God's plan has evolved to a certain extent today. When more Catholics come to believe what their life's work is, and realize that following Jesus is a commitment to do God's work, then we can believe that in several million years all people, all animals and Mother Earth herself will be living a life full of love and peace, and God's will accomplished. We often pray, "Your will be done on earth, as it is in heaven." Someday that prayer will become a reality, and Jesus will have fully returned.

Deo Gratias

Chapter 16

CLERGY & SEXUALITY

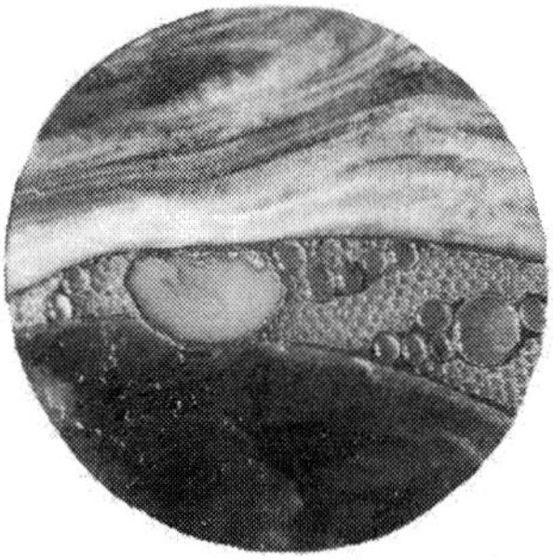

Pastoral Reflection

It seems that the media often paints a picture of the dark side of the Church. At times the articles they write are relevant and new. However, people always like to hear the dark side. It is more interesting to them.

The first thing I want to discuss is the Church's handling of sex and sexuality. I often call it "pelvic morality" because it has much to do with the pelvis. Moral theologians fill many books outlining moral theology, and what is immoral in the area of sexuality. This took a real hit back in the 1980's, when sexual abuse became well known. This is yet another example of a very dysfunctional Church. As I see it, on the one hand lay people - religious women and men - have been faithful to their commitments, and have extended themselves in their caring for others.

I am very proud of the people who build schools, and train people to teach. Most of them are shining examples of compassion, kindness and love, and how to invest one's life in elementary school, secondary school, and even college and university education. It has been caring health professionals who established hospitals, and trained doctors and nurses, who in turn cared for the sick. Healthcare has been offered to the poor and the marginalized without cost.

Then there were the families who established loving and caring homes for children, where they had safety and the opportunity to grow into healthy adults. Locally and regionally, food banks have opened up everywhere, in order to feed the hungry. Once a civic official in Peterborough told me that the Church's practice of justice and social activities saved the City thousands of dollars in welfare costs.

I know that there has been a revelation of the "shadow of the Church." There has been sexual abuse by religious brothers and sisters, and sexual assault by pastors and other religious folk. The worse part of this, has been the cover-up by Bishops who simply moved the clergy from one parish or diocese to another. As we know, the issue of sexual assault has snowballed out of control for many years.

This is not just in local parishes, but all over the world. People call the Vatican a swamp, because of what has been going on. There has been sexual activity by Cardinals, Bishops and Priests. It seems that a high percentage of our spiritual leaders, while claiming to be celibate, are actually the opposite. They have been very sexually active, and are still today. I think many of us would agree, that this behavior has to come to an end. I see it as very unfair, that these clergy should be leaders of a Christian Church. Even with the systemic evil that is in the Church hierarchy, they continue to carry on. We know these clergy will never fire themselves from their cozy jobs. If there is going to be reform in the Catholic Church, it will not come from the top down, but from the bottom up. Lay people must take this issue into their own hands.

Empowered by the Holy Spirit, they must demand that change be made, and that only men who are living a life of integrity and honesty be in charge of the Church. We know that Pope Francis is well aware of the immorality at the Vatican, and throughout the world. It is clear that he would like to clean up this mess, but he does not have the power to do so. Once again, it is going to have to happen by lay people who stand up and be counted, who protest and make their voices heard. They must have the courage to do this, and not just sit back and criticize. That will be useless. There are Catholic clergy around the world who are moral and righteous, and they are our ethical spiritual leaders.

Another area that needs to be dealt with, is the place for women in the life of the Church. We know that years ago many people interpreted the story of the garden of Eden as original sin. Not so. The balance of male power has resulted in women being discriminated against, and their gifts and talents are denied in the life of the Church. Again, this is a great injustice that cries out to heaven for it to be made right. The idea that women are inferior to men is simply wrong, wrong, wrong. The "patriarchal and misogynist attitude" among men has got to change, by emulating the mind of Christ that sees all people - men and women - as equal.

The next item which must be addressed in the life of the Church, is the very structure of the Church itself. Early on men dominated the structure of the Church, and even today we call that structure "hierarchy." The man at the top is called "Pope," the Curia is made up of men, and the Priesthood is made up of men. Many women have suffered a great deal because of the misuse of power by men in authority, and this must end if the Church is going to be true to the teachings of Jesus. I believe that if we had women Priests as part of the clergy, there would never have been such rampant abuse in the Church worldwide. Women would have spoken out, and with equal power would have been able to do something to stop it. Knowing what I do, it has been a very difficult time to be an active minister in the Catholic Church.

It is a dysfunctional Church, and I am not surprised that it has a shadow side. What I do rejoice in - even though it is very painful - is that the shadow has been exposed. Now the shadow can be dealt with, and be redeemed. However, as much as I am convinced that the people will redeem the shadow, how many will stand by their convictions and protest the hypocrisy? With the writings of the Popes, the Church has been very strong in promoting social justice throughout the world. Now the Church needs to turn its eye on itself, and practice what it preaches. The last thing I will say, is that the Church is self-destructing itself. The hierarchy is controlled by clericalism, which Pope Francis has condemned.

I invite people who really care, to pray for our Mother Church. I am Catholic and I love my Church, even with its blemishes. Many people are writing that the Church is going out of existence. If it does, I think not just the hierarchy, but all of us will be held responsible. Perhaps if the institution dies, other models of the Church will rise out of the ashes. One thing I know for sure, is that God is not going to give up on His project, which is to bring about the Kingdom of Heaven here on Earth. God has called us to join with Him in this great work. I believe it is a great honor to be called by the God of the universe to join with Him, and bring about the Kingdom of God here on Earth. I pray that before you and I die, we will join hands and hearts, and bring new life and integrity into the Catholic Church.

Deo Gracias

Chapter 17

SYSTEMIC EVIL

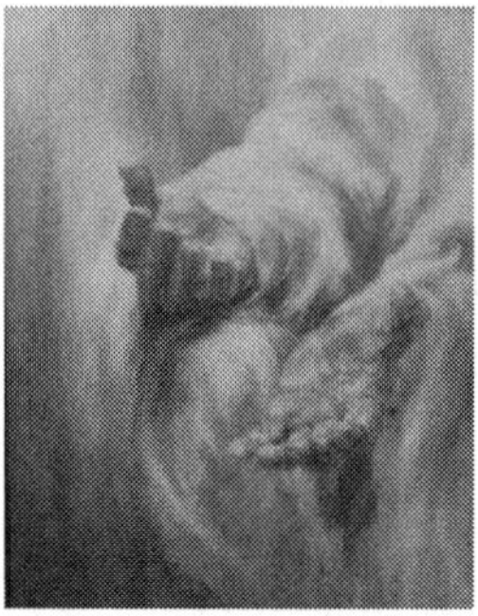

In the previous chapter I wrote about the Vatican being a swamp. I mentioned that there is corruption and immorality on a large scale. For example, sexual misbehavior, adultery, fornication, fraud, jealousy, and power games being played out by Cardinals, Bishops, Priests, and many other people living and working at the Vatican. I have learned that three of the last five Popes have been homosexuals, and have surrounded themselves with active homosexuals. The Church often describes gay men as intrinsically disordered, which shows a mindset that is totally wrong. As a result, there has been a massive effort to cover-up what was happening and "stay in the closet," but at the same time being sexually active. So many of the Cardinals, Bishops and Priests have been living a double life. Yet, they were supposed to be examples of true followers of Jesus, and live by His teachings. They were to be our spiritual leaders, and help to build a Kingdom of God on Earth. This immoral kind of lifestyle, in my opinion, makes it impossible for them to be spiritual leaders.

I have no problem with many of the men in Rome being homosexuals, but what I do object to is them living a double life. The public views them as important people in the Church, while at the same time their "double lifestyle" is wrong, and clericalism at its worst.

A hypocritical position by any spiritual leader is unacceptable. In some places, the heterosexual clergy that includes Cardinals, Bishops and Priests either have a mistress, a woman friend, or are even living with a woman and raising a family. Their way of life is completely unacceptable as spiritual leaders in the 21st century. In the Vatican and in dioceses worldwide, there is misuse of power to control lay people and to keep them disempowered, subservient, and obedient to the laws of the Church, all while ignoring the teachings of Jesus.

Pastoral Reflection

What we see is the existence of "systemic evil" in the life of the Church. As already discussed, in the fourth century Christianity became the official religion of the Roman empire, "exchanging the cross for the crown." Our use of the word crown symbolizes the new-found power of the Church in the affairs of the empire. The Church itself became structured just like the empire, with one man at the top (the Pope), second the Curia just like the Roman senators, governors in the various provinces, and the Roman army using force to keep order. The Church authorities learned from the Roman Empire how to structure the Church. The diocese received the Bishops to govern them, and Pastors were then appointed as an extension of the Bishop to govern the parish. In my opinion, this hierarchical system laid the foundation for systemic evil.

On his first Christmas address, Pope Francis made a statement indicating he was a shrewd observer of the systemic evil of his Curia. He mentioned the 15 Curia diseases including existential schizophrenia, couriers who "murder in cold blood" the reputation of their fellow cardinals, prelates who create a parallel world for themselves, the terrorism of gossip, and the terrorism of God - an alternate universe where they set aside what they teach others and live a hidden and dissolute life. Could it be any clearer? The connection between slander and double lies is now established by the most honorable irrefutable witness of all - the Pope. He was not mistaken.

What is systemic evil? Can we see it? Systemic evil appearing as structured evil is obvious in everyday life. It can appear as good, but I see it as delusional. Structural evil consists of "chains that bring us into the systemic exploitation of people." All this evil is intricate and cleverly hidden.

These chains come from outside forces that include power arrangements, ideologies, values, practices and policies – all manifesting in a systemic evil that go beyond the physical power of individuals to counter. And yet, the power arrangements and other forces that compose the Church, are humanly constructed. We also see that systemic evil is built into the very structure in society, within corporations, multinational financial institutions, governments and the Church. Men who might otherwise be powerless become a Priest, Bishop or Cardinal - part of clericalism or the clerical system - and immediately inherit power. This power is used to dominate and disempower people - especially to control them - and to exclude women and call them "dear sheep."

Many people see the Pope as powerful. And yet he is only as powerful as the clergy that defer to him, and nothing more. Power lies with the Curia that plays a big role in dominating the Church. Power lies with the Cardinals and Bishops, who misuse, oppress and dominate people. You need only to read the canon law book of the Church and the Catholic catechism, to see how clericalism has built in laws, regulations and rules that empower them, and in turn disempower the people. The behavior of the leaders of our Church that I outline, is a great sign of systemic evil. As is the manner in which so many of our Church leaders get away with it all. Even local pastors have been tyrants towards the people in their parish. Many in the pursuit of God often use power to control people. St. Thomas Aquinas wrote that nobody chooses evil, but leaders who choose evil under the disguise of good are not able to see the harm they are causing people.

The 21st century calls out for a completely different structure for the Catholic Church.

The one that we have inherited is broken, and no longer functions for the good of the people of God. Educated Catholics will no longer stand in awe of, nor be obedient to dictates from on high. The people who pay their way in the Church, expect to have a Church that is transparent. A Church of the future must include lay people having a role in the decision-making process. There are two key words which must be a part of the decision-making process - collaboration and transparency. This will be one way to rid the Church of systemic evil, and create a new model of leadership. A whole Church with moral relationships would equate to the faithful followers of Jesus and His way of life. New structure equals a new Church!

Deo Gratias

Chapter 18

GROWING UP CATHOLIC

June 1991 at the Homestead Mary Shirley Fr. Leo Barbara Charlie Patricia Gerry Audrey Absent: Rita Richard Carmel

A family gathering at Fr. Leo's house in Asphodel Township

As I reflect on my years growing up, there was much joy, laughter and humor, and the goodness that enabled one to appreciate moving from a child to a teen. However, the one part of growing up that was not joyful or healthy, was religion. My family grew up in an Irish Catholic community, where there was a communal way of thinking and acting. There were two elementary schools in the community - Catholic or Public. My family all attended the public school because it was a closer walking distance, and this was the will of our father. Every August the Pastor would appear at our house, asking us to attend the Catholic school. Each year my father's answer was the same "No." We continued to attend the public school as well as the public high school. When it came to high school I became more and more bored, and really detested going to school.

Yet I went every day, because the alternative was to work on the farm, and I did not want that. As I reflect on the Church of my youth, I see that it was very unhealthy for people. It was a Church that made people fear God.

Later in life I heard a psychologist talk about "Catholic guilt." There was a reason for the guilt. The Church of my youth taught the absolutes of obedience to God and the Ten Commandments. Over a period of 2000 years, the Church adopted many rules and regulations that made it impossible to be good. To motivate people to be good, we were reminded that when we died God would judge the living and the dead, and God had a book containing all the bad things we had ever done in our life. One of the worst things I remember, is that sin was everywhere. It seemed that no matter what you thought or did, or what you did or did not do, it was probably sinful.

We were taught that baptism was absolutely necessary for salvation. I often asked what happened to all the people who were not Christian and not baptized! The whole set-up did not seem fair to me. In my youth I thought that if I was a bad person headed for hell, I might as well be bad. And in many ways I was a disobedient teenager. The Pastor kept reminding us that everyone needed to go to confession, and make their Easter duty. Therefore, our mother would drive us to the Church every month for confession, which I detested. At the time I did not like the Pastor, and having to go to confession to him was distasteful. The older I got, the more I realized that I would have to use my powers of thought to survive religion.

Looking back, I see a Church that was joyless, sin-focused and guilt-ridden, and that promoted the idea of a judgmental God. I needed a God of love and compassion, not a distant sky God, but a God close to me. This God enabled me to live a life that was meaningful - not just for myself but for the good of others. English poet Francis Thompson wrote a poem entitled "The Hound of Heaven." This hound of heaven was God, whom I had met.

We had come to know each other, and I saw him as a God who dwelled within me and all around me. This God knew me, and called me by my name. And this God loved me unconditionally, with all my mistakes and sins. I did not fear this God, and I did not feel guilty that I was not good enough, because I realized I did not have to be "good enough." I just needed to be kind, loving and compassionate, and work for social justice. Since I am a Priest of the living God, I wanted to serve the people of God first and foremost, and to not focus on obedience to laws or rules.

Pastoral Reflection

After about 60+ years of ministry, I see changes that must come to our Church if it is going to serve the people of God. There are things that need to be corrected, and I am going to list a few of them here. There are others that I am not going to list here. The first is our Faith Story, or our belief system as it is sometimes called. We know that our Faith Story has been developing for over 2000 years. Some of it is very good, and some of it is simply wrong. Even Vatican Council II and most of its documents, are obsolete today. During the last fifty years scientists have brought forward new discoveries and ideas, and have shown how technology has become integral to our world and culture, often to the exclusion of God.

Words like evolution, new cosmology, new biology, quantum physics, and artificial intelligence are now embedded into our language and conversation. People have stopped believing many of the tenets of the traditional faith story. People no longer give blind obedience to doctrine, dogma or canon law. We are living with the first generation of educated Catholics who are critical thinkers, think for themselves, and take personal responsibility for their spirituality. Another change I feel we need in our Church is the role of women. The misinterpretation of the Garden of Eden is another item that needs to be corrected. St. Augustine used it as a foundation for his teaching on original sin.

Today's scripture scholars disagree with the teachings of men being superior to women, and women being subservient to men. This inequality has played itself out by preventing them from having a part in the structure of the Church. We know that women were very close to Jesus, walked with him, supported him, and ministered to people. Women were a major part of the early Church. However, male clergy ruled, and barred women from full participation in the life of the Church, especially ordination to the Priesthood.

Today we have Priests coming from all over the world - good men - but their cultures are different, and they find it difficult to be effective in our local ministry. Women are equal to men in every way, and diversity is part of the Church. Despite discrimination women can choose careers such as social justice, education, healthcare, prayer animators, Church workers, pastoral care in parishes, hospitals or prisons, and yet they can still be diminished, criticized and dominated by male clergy. As if their many gifts and talents are not at the service of the people of God. This has to end, as women have a divine right to be active in the life of the Church. This means they must be treated as equals by the clergy, be part of the decision-making, and how money is spent. And if they wish to be ordained to the Priesthood and serve as pastors in parishes, then it is their right.

In the doctrine God was understood to be up in heaven, and sinful people were here on Earth. If they were good, they might receive a favorable judgment from a punitive God. The Incarnation tells us very clearly that the son of God became human in Jesus. And the Incarnation of God in the sacrament represents people on Planet Earth from the very beginning until the end of time - they are God become human. One of the most difficult things to do, is to change minds and acknowledge that we are God become human, that God dwells within us and all around us. Our God is not a distant God sitting on a throne up in the sky but is down here with us.

God is everywhere, and there is nowhere we can go to hide from God. We are not sinners in the eyes of God. God loves us unconditionally no matter what. God knows us and calls us by name. I teach that God is the source and substance of all that is. God is a God of unconditional love that does not take offence.

I know that many live with guilt and fear of punishment, and yet the Spirit has revealed to us that God does not take offence, and so we have nothing to worry about. Nothing can separate us from the love of God. It seems to me that we need to make some changes, on not only how we see God, but also on how we worship God in the celebration of the Eucharist. During the Eucharistic prayers we proclaim that the Mass is a sacrifice, a way of being reconciled with God, and of making peace with an angry God. This teaching is obsolete and false.

I know that congregations around the world have declined as people no longer attend Mass. In 1958 when I started my ministry, 80% of Catholics in Canada attended Mass weekly. My guess is that it is down to about 10-15% today. This is true in many countries. The Church has been declining since the late 1970's. I think of the staff members in hundreds of schools educating the youth with love and compassion. There are also thousands of Catholic hospitals throughout the world where the sick are cared for, with holistic care that includes physical and mental aspects, but also the spiritual. There are many Catholics working as pastoral care workers in parishes, chaplains in hospitals and prisons, and for social justice. This is a Church that is alive, and one that we can be proud of.

As I reflect on the leadership in the Church, it leaves me with a sense of hopelessness and helplessness. The hierarchy of the Church is a political machine that protects its own. You have to wonder if the sexually active Cardinals, Bishops and Priests really believe in God, and if Jesus is the Lord of their life? I doubt it.

It reminds me of Jesus who looked at the religious leaders of His day and called them hypocrites or, "whited sepulchers filled with dead man's bones." My guess is that He would say the same thing today.

There needs to be a cleaning of the house, and an infusion of young people committed to the service of people and God, as the number one priority in their lives. Anything short of this will not restore our trust in the clergy. It would not surprise me if small home Churches, faith-sharing groups, bible study groups, and justice-making groups, etc. will replace big Churches and the elaborate living quarters of Cardinals and Bishops. The question of the work facing us today is, what is God doing? I really believe that the Church has lost its way. God is still here and active, and God will inspire people to collaborate with all of creation to bring about the Kingdom of God here on Earth. I know I may never see it, but that is my prayer and my hope. I believe that God will never give up on the human race, even though some of us have given up on God at this time in history.

Deo Gratias

Chapter 19

OUR MASS

When people come to Sunday Eucharist, they come to worship with various needs and hopes. We know that many people are carrying heavy burdens, and living in a world where there is a great deal of fear and anxiety. There is always the hope that somehow the Sunday worship will strengthen people, and give them courage and hope so they can meet the challenges of the coming week. When I worked for the School Board, the feedback I got from teachers opened my eyes to what was really going on. Many teachers told me that they no longer attended Sunday Mass in their Parish because they found it boring - it was the same old thing every Sunday. They also complained about the lack of hospitality when they attended Mass. No one there seemed to welcome them, and if they did not show up, no one seemed to miss them.

Teachers have studied theological courses and have attended university, so they have a new way of interpreting scripture. Yet the same old interpretation continues to appear in the Sunday homily. Many teachers told me that when they left the Church after Mass and drove home, they felt anger and disappointment.

It was then they realized that they were in a negative state, and decided to stop going to Mass to protect themselves.

As the years went by, by working with members of the community we tried to use creativity and innovation when designing our Sunday liturgies. Many factors have a role in the diminishment of attendance at Mass on Sunday. Some pastors have told me that while we have six parishes in the City of Peterborough, two would be enough. Now we must keep in mind, that there is much more to Christianity than going to Mass. In the past, attending Mass meant you were a good Catholic and had a good chance of getting to heaven. Missing Mass was a mortal sin and people risked going to hell. This makes it seem as though people came to Mass because of fear and guilt. Pope Francis told the Bishops and the Priests to put an end to the Latin Mass being celebrated in the Churches. Yet, we know that many Bishops have told the Priests that they will continue to say the Latin Mass. This in itself is counter-productive. It tells people that you do not have to obey the Pope. It also tells us that this regressive behavior of presiding at, and attending Latin Mass, is going back to a time long gone. We call this behavior "nostalgia neurosis."

Pastoral Reflection

It seems to me that somehow we have to bring forth the idea that Christianity is not simply going to Mass every Sunday. Yes, attending Mass means that people expect well-researched and well delivered homilies that really give people food for thought. It must be a liturgy in which people can participate, and put their gifts and talents to the service of the larger community. Often many people in a Parish do not know the other parishioners, and unless the parish is alive and brings people together, it will not be a community. It will simply be a bunch of individuals gathering for a Mass. Parishioners must create a Liturgy Committee, and must meet at least once a month to plan the liturgy for the next month - coordinating the music ministry with the scripture readings and have well-trained and spirit-filled lectors.

In many parish Churches, everyone is too serious and there is no joy. No one feels nourished, and many do not return. As I said, there is a lot more to Christianity than attending Mass on Sunday. Very often religion focuses on morality or immorality. But the point of Christianity is to help people to live a way of life, as that taught and lived by Jesus.

True reflection on scripture helps to build our faith. Christians must remember that they are called to do God's work, and God's work is to build the Kingdom of God here on Earth. Now that we have combined science with faith, the Parish must also do the same and not keep repeating the same old images, scripture readings and moralistic homilies because their relevance is gone. We know the leaders of the Church, the hierarchy, are so far behind evolution that for them the train has left the station and they are not on it. We also know that Catholic people have been so brainwashed, they feel they have no real voice, or no real authority to stand up and speak the truth.

In our baptism we are empowered to do the work of God. Today if our Church is going to survive and do God's work the people in the pews must take ownership of their power, and accept the responsibility that the people are meant to be the engine that runs the Church. Being silent, choosing not to speak up, failing to organize and protest, having reluctance to challenge the Pastor or the Bishop of the Diocese and demand a larger role in the life of the Church, will result in the Church becoming even more and more irrelevant. Even now I see the Church in the West as moving into a living death.

There are many Catholics who are indeed taking ownership of their empowerment. They are no longer silent, and are refusing to be oppressed by clergy. It seems to me that our Church is going to survive, but in a completely different form. The whole world must experience a tremendous transition to a new reality. The Church has been left behind because we have simply not kept up with the times. Seminarians must be taught how to combine science and the gospel - this is an absolute.

While a few people are still attending Mass in the Church, the Priest must educate himself on quantum mechanics and physics if he is going to be able to teach people about the present and possible future. We are people of the future, not the past. I think part of this, is all of us waking up and realizing that God needs us to do Her work. This is the way creation has arranged it, and like it or not, it is the way it is. If we are able to see that this is the way, then perhaps we will wake up and hopefully swing into action, without being afraid of the consequences.

In the world today we are seeing a Great Awakening. We are living in a Global Village and science has shown us that we are an interrelated and interdependent species. We are one with all of creation. Some futurists are talking about the repercussions of artificial intelligence and robots. They tell us that artificial intelligence means that fewer people will work for a living, and many people will never work throughout their lives. So how will society help everyone find meaning and purpose in their lives? The unemployed will need a guaranteed annual wage so that they can live with dignity.

Deo Gratias

Chapter 20

SO-CALLED CATHOLIC GUILT

When I think of Catholic guilt, I have come to realize that guilt is part of the human condition. There are many sources that drive us to experience guilt - parents, education, religion, and even later in life events that tend to make us feel less than good enough. Psychology calls it the "internal critical parent." Some are able to free themselves from the critical parent, while another may need assistance to be less judgmental of themselves, and be free of guilt. Guilt is counter-productive. I am not surprised, as over the years I listened to Catholics who were wanting and needing to speak of their guilt. By seeking healing, they were able to experience freedom and much more joy in life.

When I was growing up it seemed that sin was everywhere. First it was the original sin, then venial sin, and finally mortal sin. Of course, the threat was that if you died with a mortal sin on your soul, God would judge you and send you to hell. Hell was a place of everlasting punishment, and not very appealing. I remember my pastor often criticized pleasure seekers when he was preaching on Sunday. As a teenager I know I was a pleasure seeker! I felt pleasure in driving the tractor, I felt pleasure being with my friends and enjoying life, and I felt pleasure in playing sports. Obviously, I soon learned that I was a sinner.

We were taught that Jesus came to die on the cross for us, and we should be appreciative of Him dying so He could take away our sins. Once a month, one of the things we always did on Saturday evenings was go to the village Church. On the way, I remember my mother pointing to each one of us in the car and reminding us of our sins, so that we would be prepared for confession. I did not enjoy going to confession, and many a time I had to make up some sins to tell. Naturally I confessed little sins, that would not cause the Priest to get too upset with me.

Pastoral Reflection

Soon after I became a Priest I saw the concept in action, of each person being a sinner and having to go to confession every week. Also thinking they could not go to Holy Communion without confessing their sins first, was causing people a lot of stress. They were filled with fear for their salvation, while carrying a burden of guilt from which there was no relief. I remember at Sacred Heart Parish, there were confessions every Saturday afternoon and evening for four hours. I soon discovered was that it was the same sinners every week, and they were not improving in their spiritual life or their behavior.

As a good Catholic, I thought this was the way it was, to be a Catholic. This was the way that Catholics function, and I was part of the system. I was a happy person and did not usually call people sinners. Yes, there was sin in the world but mostly it was corporate sin, the sin of injustice, or the sin of oppression. The sin of people getting richer and richer, while the poor were getting poorer and poorer. There was the sin of violence, especially against women, and this was particularly repugnant to me as I loved my seven sisters. At the time I did some pondering, and came to the realization that I needed to change both my idea and image of God. As I read the Gospels, I clearly saw that the writers offered me an image of a God of unconditional love, a God who dwelled among us, and within us. I realized that creation is the Body of God, and we can see God if we open our eyes to a God who does not punish or judge anyone.

I realized that I had a God who loved me unconditionally, a God who did not take offence at my mistakes, a God who did not punish me. The very air I breathe is the breath of the Spirit of God. A fish in the ocean never asks where the water is, so I do not ask where God is, because I live in God and God lives in me. And yet there are consequences for this fundamental belief, about a loving and caring God. The first thing it means is that I, and all other people, are not sinners. We are God's beloved, and we live in a viable loving relationship with God and all of God's creation - the Earth, all the greenery on the Earth, all the birds in the air, all living creatures and all people. God loves us simply because we are his sons and daughters.

Many years ago, an old pastor told me that if he was to live his life over again, he would preach only one sermon. He said the topic of his sermon would be God's unconditional love for all. If people were able to believe that God is with them, that He lives within them and loves them, they will be able to avoid a lot of struggles. I often think of Catholics about to die, who know they are going to face their final exam before a punitive God. It would be fearful enough to believe they were dying, without the fear that God would find them a sinner and send them to hell. What a terrible experience! When it comes to salvation, the word is confusing to many. For many people salvation means being good, repenting for your sins, having a Priest at your side when you are dying, and then maybe going to heaven. Salvation comes from the Latin word "Salus" meaning health and wellness. Thus you can see that it has a lot to do with the physical realm and our bodies. Salvation is a word that is active, and touches the lives of people in this world - not in the afterlife. When we believe that God loves us unconditionally, we know that we are already in heaven.

However, we also know that we live in a world where there is war and bloodshed, a lack of peace, great injustice and oppression, and people who have too much money, and others who don't have enough. It seems as if Catholics are trapped in the belief that salvation enables us to get to heaven, and yet this is not true.

The Kingdom of God is a way of life for the here and now. Jesus made that very clear, as He walked among the people in His day. Read the Gospels and study the words of Jesus, and you will see the points I am making. When people in need came to Jesus, the Scripture says that Jesus was moved with compassion and ministered to them. Jesus fed the hungry and cured the sick. He did not retaliate or seek revenge. Jesus taught a great message of justice and peace. We know all about our family and our bloodlines, and how precious these relationships are. By baptism we join a larger spiritual family committed to Jesus and His way of life, committed to doing our best to bring about what He called the Kingdom of God here on Earth.

The spiritual family to which we belong is our first family, and our much smaller human family is our second family. Very few people understand the significance of belonging to the spiritual family of God. As a result, they remain fixated on the human family and what they have to offer, and our obligations to them. Remember, Jesus said to His apostles, "If you want to be one of My followers, leave your families and follow me." Jesus also said, "If you want to be my follower you have to be committed. Anyone who puts their hands to the plough and looks back, is not fit for the Kingdom of God."

At times people wanted to join Jesus as one of His disciples, but Jesus said they were not ready. They were not ready to make a commitment and so He declined. Christian spirituality is based on a commitment to follow Jesus and His way of life. It is our humanity, our physical well-being, our growth and transformation into the best person we can be, that means an ever-growing capacity for loving yourself, other people, Earth Community and God. It was once written, "Love God and do what you will," so our lives are meant to be inspired, motivated, and strengthened by our love for all of creation. We can be a part of the process towards the Omega point to which we are all moving, and will do so for several million more years.

Deo Gratias

Chapter 21

THE GREAT AWAKENING

The Miracle of Birth

Spiritual writers have written about the Great Awakening in the last fifty years. The First Awakening was primarily in the 60's and 70's, when most of us are old enough to remember. The first and most obvious one was the sexual awakening and the freedom for sexual activity. There was also the drug awakening, although it was primarily marijuana and psychedelic drugs. There were also many social awakenings with people watching television and travelling the world, that added to their experiences and expanded their lives. The Second Awakening came with the invention of technology, and the worldwide web. For young people attending college and university, they become educated and trained to think for themselves. As a result of thinking for themselves many of the young and educated have turned away from the traditions and the wisdom of their elders.

The Third Awakening took place with the explosion of the internet and computers. Society changed radically with a new interest and concern for the environment, and a tremendous movement toward social justice and peace work.

The Fourth Awakening has been taking place in the last number of years, as the world has been transformed into a global village through travel, the internet and people deciding for themselves what is right or wrong. The traditional religions of the world have been the big losers. This is particularly true in the Churches in the West, as people simply voted with their feet and left the Church. Everything is moving forward, and every aspect of society is experiencing evolution except the institutions of religion. This is particularly true of the Catholic Church. It has often been observed that the people who are attending weekend Masses wearing masks, have grey hair and are senior citizens. I saw this beginning in the late 70's but I did not recognize it as the start of the Great Awakening, which has been a movement of people away from the Church.

When I began my Ministry in 1958, 80% of Catholics attended Mass on Sunday. Now we are down to about 10% -15%, which is a very substantial loss. Things have changed in society, and young people in particular do not attend Church for Sunday Mass. By young people I mean people under fifty. The iPad and iPhone have become extremely important. Computers are created to work faster and faster, and with Facebook, Zoom and other apps people are able to communicate all over the world. There is often a major conflict between the traditional and the progressives, between those on the left and those on the right. We see our Church becoming very divided as Catholics choose the left or the right, with little tolerance for each other. We see where theology has taken great steps forward, as scientists provide theologians with information and knowledge about the universe that culminates in the new emerging faith story. This emerging story focuses on spirituality and spiritual growth, and not so much on doctrine and dogma. The Great Awakening shows that people are rising up around the world toward a new and different way. Relationships, multi-culturalism, and social values have all radically changed. There is also a whole new awakening to the value and importance of the Earth. The Earth is sick, and many people are sick as a result of living on planet Earth.

People are becoming aware of this, and are saying that they need to invest more time and energy into caring for the environment. They are awakening to the harm that is being done from the use of fossil fuels, and to find new forms of renewable energy. The electric car is one of the partial answers. Evolution shows that society must become one of collaboration and cooperation throughout the world. There are issues that we must deal with, such as climate warming, care of the Earth, needless violence, poverty and food equity. As we move into 2022, these are some of the issues, and it is through collaboration that the human race will be able to address them, and bring justice to our world.

Pastoral Reflection

As I look back over the last 50 years, I have seen the diminishment of our Church. It began very slowly, with a few people here and there simply dropping out. Then it became very rapid, as people voted with their feet and walked away. I know that many young adults found the Sunday service boring. I heard those words over and over. As I mentioned before, many talked about the lack of hospitality in the Church building as they arrived through the doors. Many talked about the slow and meaningless music that was still being used in the 21st century. Many also made references to the scripture readings, which they found to be out-of-date. There were also a lot of comments about how homilies were irrelevant. The common phrase I heard over and over was that they were not feeling supported when they attended the Sunday Eucharist. They were looking for a community, and it was not in the Church.

People in North America, South America and Europe have been leaving the Church by the millions. Unfortunately, it seems that our leaders are not able to find ways to bring about the change that would continue to attract them. During the pandemic when the Churches were practically closed, many people found they liked sleeping in on Sunday morning. They felt more rested, and decided they could get along just fine without going to Mass. So this situation begs the question, what is God doing?

Where is God? Why does God not bring those millions of people back to the Church? I think one of the problems is that the Church has lost its way. It no longer leads people to a living dynamic relationship with God. Very few parishes offer people anything other than Sunday Mass. This is not enough. People are looking for spiritual nourishment. They are looking for food that gives life. I know from my own training in the seminary, that we were not trained to be spiritual directors. It was taken for granted that if people attended Mass and lived a good life, all would be well. We can see this was a big mistake.

We are living in the age of a Great Awakening, and this is very true in the area of spirituality. It seems that God no longer needs or wants the Churches as they now exist. However, God does need people to do His work here on Earth. The work of God is to bring about the Kingdom of God, and we have not made that a focus of our spirituality. As a matter of fact, this notion, this understanding, that we are here to do the work of God has nothing to do with being good. The call of the gospel is to do God's work first and foremost.

I have already talked about the Great Awakening, and with it, seeing presence in the action of God. God is doing a new thing in our world. We have extremely well-qualified spiritual writers who are providing us with food for our soul, and growth and transformation. This is essential for the people of God to develop their spirituality, and to keep up with the times in which we live. The new spirituality is still the same law of love, the love of God, the love of self, and the love of our neighbor. Do you love the Earth, do you see that all who live on Earth are sacred, and are to be treated with respect and love?

What do I see God doing? First of all, we have to realize that the Incarnation is real, we are God become human. I look out in our world and I see people finding new ways to look after their own spirituality, so they can grow and be transformed.

I see in the Great Earth Awakening that people are moving forward in small groups like Bible study, faith-sharing groups, book clubs, social justice, and peace in the world. There are environmentalists who are working to save the Earth from destruction. There are people choosing to live a much simpler life. There are people building communities of faith. Many now emphasize the importance of relationships, with other people and all of Earth Community.

As I look out upon our beautiful Earth, I see a Great Awakening in the lives and hearts of people who are finding a new path, and a new way of nurturing and growing in their spiritual life. At the present time they are led by those who belong in the community, not by the clergy. I don't know if this is the end of clericalism, with a new movement being developed by lay leadership (which is how the Church originally began). As I think of the future I do so with hope. I am optimistic because I see and believe that we are spiritual people. People will be inspired by the Holy Spirit to grow in their love for God, and be strengthened by doing God's work as they build the Kingdom of God here on Earth. As I see this new movement, many are pushing back and trying to put a halt to it, as they want go back to the old ways. We certainly see this with clergy who want to go back to traditional Latin Masses, and other spiritual exercises from the past. We should never be surprised at pushback, as it is the nature of human beings who are afraid of change and the future. However, I am confident that the Holy Spirit will be much too strong for those who try to put a halt to growth.

It seems to me that the Church of the future will not need elaborate and beautiful buildings. Most of the gatherings will happen in offices, homes, coffee shops, restaurants and other small spaces. We are living in very opportune times. Evolution is carrying all of creation into the future. We are all evolving, and institutions that stand still will simply die. People will be led and inspired by the Holy Spirit - as was the early Church. This is the strongest argument I have for living with hope and confidence, for a whole new way to come together and do God's work. By doing this we will prepare the world for future generations. Deo Gratias

Chapter 22

A SPIRITUAL FAMILY

As a Christian people we often talk about community, and how important and valuable a living, loving and life-giving community is to the well-being of the people. The need to belong is fundamental to all humans. When we read the Gospels, we see how Jesus clearly reveals he has a project, that can work in such a way it will bring about the Kingdom of God. He is going to invite people to join His team. People will embark on a journey to teach a whole new way of thinking, a whole new way of seeing reality, and a new way of living and behaving.

For people to suddenly move into a dynamic life, is a leap of faith. People are going about the ordinary business of living, and they deeply value their blood family and the relationships they cherish. Their worldview is often characterized by consumerism and misuse of power, and living in a world of violence and hate, while seeking revenge and retaliation.

There is great injustice in the land, as we see the rich getting richer and the poor getting poorer. The gospel tells us that the religious leaders of the day are misusing their prestige for power. There were many poor and marginalized people at the time of Jesus, and He moved with compassion to minister to the poor. Jesus was very critical of the life lived by the religious leaders of His day. He also showed His critical side, when He said that they were hypocrites who were exploiting the poor.

Pastoral Reflection

This chapter is going to challenge your thinking, and discover if you are able and willing to see with new eyes - to see the big picture - and what Jesus was actually doing in order for his work to continue. Jesus established what we call a spiritual family. At one time, Jesus was making a name for Himself by teaching and healing. However, not everyone agreed with Him, and there were rumors about His mental health. His mother and father knew He was in Capernaum, so they went there to take Him home. When they showed up at the house, it was filled with people listening to the teachings of Jesus. The word was passed along to Jesus that His mother, father and brothers were outside and wanted to be with Him. They was His blood family. But Jesus would not go with them. He was with His spiritual family, a new family to which He was committed. This spiritual family would take precedence over his blood family.

At other locations people came and asked Jesus if they could join him. He replied that it would have to be right away. One said, "No, I have to go home and bury my father." Another said, "I just bought a new farm." Another said, "I have just been married." They were talking about responsibilities toward their blood family. At that point, Jesus told them that they had too strong an attachment to their blood family, and were not ready or free enough to join His spiritual family. We know that the twelve apostles responded to Jesus' call immediately, along with others, and particularly women who were using their own money to provide food and lodging. Slowly but surely, the new spiritual family grew, with commitment and strong in numbers. Jesus was always open and honest with people. He said that if they followed Him, they had to make a commitment to live in His spiritual family, and this would cost them. As a matter of fact, Jesus told them that if they were going to be faithful followers, they had to be prepared to carry the cross of growth and transformation. Now by his use of the word cross, He did not mean crucifixion, although that would come later.

What Jesus meant, was to live a life of integrity and love, reaching out to the poor and the marginalized every day, and being prepared for criticism and persecution. The cross was a symbol of living each day as a life of love. Jesus also made it clear that if you made a commitment to a loving God, you would live in a spiritual family, meaning that your blood family would come second to your spiritual family.

Today as we are going through a great transition in the Church and Church life, we need to hear about, and to be awakened to, the spiritual family that is created by Jesus. There are a few people who have given their whole life to God and Jesus. Do you put your gifts and talents in the service of other people? Jesus wants people who live in the spiritual family to enjoy life. When we become members of the spiritual family of Jesus, the purpose of our life is very clear. That to live in such a way, by word and deed, that will bring about the Kingdom of God.

The question is, are you willing to be a viable and loving and caring person in God's spiritual family? To say "yes" is to make a commitment.

Deo Gracias

Chapter 23

THE EMERGING NEW FAITH STORY

Most of what I have included in my previous chapters has arisen out of my study and research on the emerging new Faith Story. First is the recognition that we need a new Faith Story, that grabs our heart and soul in the 21st century. The traditional faith story is primarily built on the belief of a three-tier universe. It is a cosmology that holds that the Earth is flat, that the underworld is beneath the Earth, and that God lives and reigns supreme in the heavens. As a result of this three-tier universe, we have a distant God presiding in the dome above, looking down upon humankind and all life here on Earth. In the traditional faith story, humanity is basically separated from God. This theme also appears in the teaching that not only is there a distant God, but also that humankind, by the sin of Adam and Eve, has cut itself off from God. In the traditional faith story, God is not an attractive God. God is a God of authority, a God of requirements, a God who will judge, condemn and punish. He is a God that needs a sacrifice to atone for the sins of humankind, and this can only be done by the shedding of blood by Jesus on Good Friday.

Down through the centuries, diverse theological conclusions, or theories, were added to the traditional faith story. And yet, the vast majority of Catholics in the West no longer believe in this faith story and find it irrelevant. This is one of the reasons why many Catholics have voted with their feet. Today most of our Catholic Churches cater to older people, and yet we are living with a contemporary generation of educated Catholics.

The emerging New Story is bringing us closer to the teachings of Jesus. Jesus stressed the importance of Metanoia, which is a radical change of mind and worldview. Many of the stories of Jesus are meant to change our worldview, and see our faith in a new light. This in itself is a sign that Jesus knew about evolution, although they did not have a word for it at the time. We see today that science and theology must work together to provide us with a living philosophy of life for 2022. Science without theology often feels without soul. And yet theology without science is simply outdated, and of no use to the people of the world. Jesus, born of the Virgin Mary, suffered under Pontius Pilate. He was crucified, died and was buried, and on the third day He rose from the dead. By contrast, the New Story is relational, and it is a love story that reads, "Love your neighbor as yourself," or "Love one another as I have loved you," or "Do unto others as you would have them do unto you."

Pastoral Reflection

As a cradle Catholic I began my journey in life believing everything that the Church taught. I swallowed the Baltimore catechism in its entirety, and never critiqued it. I went through seven years of study in St. Augustine's Seminary, even though I had some doubts about the teachings we were not allowed to question. If a person questioned any part of the dogma, they were sent home. I was in active Church ministry for about six months, when I realized that that the traditional faith story was becoming irrelevant for many people. I saw that its teaching was obsolete, yet I did not know what the alternative could be.

It was at this point that I decided to become a lifelong student. I firmly believed that as a religious leader I must be competent, and constantly update my thinking, teaching and preaching. Even today after 64+ years of ministry I am still a diligent student, studying God and the things of God. I see many Catholics who have grown up, matured, and are able to think for themselves. This is a good thing. They are able to critique the various dogmas and doctrines that have been proposed by the institutional Church.

The fact that Pope Francis is calling for a synod, asking for the opinions of Catholics worldwide, is a sign that he recognizes that the Church is of the people of God, not just the clergy. If the Church is going to survive and experience renewal, the voice of the people must be heard. What follows is my description of the new emerging faith story.

First, many of us experienced Vatican Council with its innovation, thought and action. However, the Vatican Council became obsolete when scientific discoveries were introduced to the world. The first concept to disappear was the three-tier universe. The new cosmology became the way to see the cosmos and the universe. The new cosmology is like the hinge on the door, which offers many new theological and spiritual ideas. The new cosmology tells us that creation is organic. Everything in existence is inter-related with everything else. All is one. It means that humans are inter-connected in relationship. It also means that humans are in relationship with Earth Community, which includes humans as part of nature. Thus all beings are in relationship with nature, with trees, ecotones and diverse landscapes. It means we are all in a relationship with Mother Earth, from which all life originated. It is Mother Earth who sustains us, and provides all the elements and nutrients that living things need to survive, and thrive.

The new emerging Faith Story tells us that creation is the Body of God. I have come to realize that we live in God, and God lives in me and all of creation. I have often said that the fish in the ocean do not ask, "Where is the water?" And yet people continue to ask, "Where is God?"

The response I give, is that creation is the Body of God, and if you want to see, hear, feel, walk, or smell the Divine then open all your senses and walk in nature. There you will experience the presence and beauty of God. We hear people asking "where is God?" The correct response is that creation is the body of God, and to know "the sacred' you must open your eyes. All is right before you in the presence of God, and in all God's glory and beauty. This is why it is so important for our spiritual lives, to spend time in nature, and allow nature to educate us about the presence of God.

Christmas is a celebration of the Incarnation of Jesus in human form. The Son of God became man, and this is the Christmas story, the Incarnation of Jesus. The emerging new faith story tells us that we are people of the Incarnation - not just Jesus - but all people worldwide whether they know it or not. Our God is not a distant God, but a God of intimacy, who has unconditional love for all of us. We are God's Beloved. We are not sinners who need Jesus to die on the cross for us. In the new faith story, science reinforces all of this and more. The new faith story has exploded with a powerful big bang, putting in motion the process of evolution that has been working through the years - nearly 14,000,000,000 years - which brings us to where we are today.

Life began on planet Earth about five billion years ago, long before the story of Adam and Eve came on the scene. We must keep in mind that the Adam and Eve story is not scientific. It is a true story and needs proper interpretation. The emerging new faith story tells us very clearly that God is with us, and in some mysterious way lives within us, and we live in God. This means that all life is sacred, and no one is excluded. All are equal, especially women and men. The animals and plant life are sacred. Mother Earth the mother of us all, is the most sacred, and deserves to be treated as a loving mother who gives us unconditional love, and sustains us in life. Humans need to stop polluting the air and water, and destroying the environment, as it is an offence against a loving God.

We need to live by the new faith story, so that we can act as living and caring keepers of our home, Mother Earth. Evolution means that creation is happening every moment of the day. The story of hope, faith and relevance must continue to evolve far into the future, as we continue to combine science with faith and spirituality.

Unfortunately, the institutional Church does not support the evolution of the new faith story. The traditional story is filled with control, perpetuated by the power of the clergy and the hierarchy. Fear, guilt, the threat of judgment and the possibility of being sent to hell, enables people to be controlled and disempowered.The new story is the very opposite. It is a story that empowers the people of God to be all they can be as human beings. It is a story that sets people free to make their own moral and behavioral choices. In fact, they are told that they are to follow their own conscience in facing moral decisions.

As we read the signs of the time, it seems that in the West the institutional Church is in big trouble, with the loss of so many people simply walking away and finding new ways to nourish their spiritual life. It is no longer within the framework of large gatherings, but rather in small groups where people gather to deepen their relationship with God and the Holy Spirit. For example, faith-sharing groups, bible study groups, social justice groups and peace-making groups, including the outreach to the hungry, the poor and the homeless. These are the choices that people are making, since they do not find anything in their local parish to nourish their spirituality. Having left their local parish, they have to find other means to grow, as a people of God.

Thanks to the internet, the global village has become a powerful means to nourish spirituality. People can belong to groups halfway around the world, and draw nourishment and teachings from their participation in various cultures and life experiences different from their own. This is only a small aspect about the emerging new Faith Story. There is so much more.

The combining of science, faith and spirituality has created a powerful narrative that can make a big difference in the lives of people, animals and nature, and especially Mother Earth. We know that a sick Earth will produce sick people, which contributes to more sickness. The new story is very powerful in Her message of loving creation, that creation is sacred and must be lived with respect and love.

Today, many environmentalists are working hard to correct the violence that has been done to Mother Earth. To neglect the environment, is to do so at our peril. I urge the readers of this chapter, especially those who have walked away from the Church, to research the new faith story and realize what a beautiful and powerful story it is. It is a story about love - the most important teaching of Jesus - and that religion is not rules and regulations. It is living in love as best as we can, to create justice not just for people but for our entire Earth Community, and finally to walk humbly with Our God.

Deo Gratias

Chapter 24

EPEKIA

One day I was having lunch with several Priests, and one of the questions posed was, "What moral principles do we use in order to make decisions in ministry?" It was a thought-provoking question that I carried away with me, and decided to search for the answer. Very often, faced with a dilemma the answer will be clear. I remember that my response was not clear at that point, and I had to turn to various moral principles upon which to make my decision.

One example I ran into frequently, was officiating at a mass in a funeral home. In Church law this is not allowed. The experience I had when celebrating my first mass influenced my decision. I remember there was a pause in the liturgy, and I heard a voice within my heart speak very clearly. The voice said, "Father Leo I want you to put people first." My response was straight to the point. I thought to myself, "God, I will always put people first, and will not blindly obey Church rules." I made that as a solemn promise to God, and I have acted on that promise many times.

In pastoral ministry, I have always endeavored to put people first, and never climb the ladder into legalism. During my years of ministry I have only had one Bishop who put people first. The others were very legalistic. I cannot remember the countless times I was reprimanded by a Bishop, yet I continued to do what I believed was the right thing. There is a saying that goes, "Don't ask for permission but later on ask for forgiveness." I refused to ask for forgiveness because I felt in my heart that I was being true to God, and that I was already doing the right thing by ignoring the rules, just as Jesus did. I felt that love should always triumph over legalism, and for that I would never ask forgiveness.

Pastoral Reflection

Two Priest-Professors with doctorate degrees came from Buffalo to teach at the seminary for two years. They were up-to-date in their thinking, and very progressive in their worldview. They taught me some ministry principles which I have never forgotten, and as a result I have been able to serve the people of God when rules were in the way of their freedom.

The first principle known as "the moral principle of double affect" means that when on the horns of a dilemma and both choices are good, one chooses one and acts on it, knowing that the other side of the equation will create harm. This principle is very helpful, especially in a hospital when an operation can indeed restore a person to health, but could also have side-effects. Many consciences were set at peace by acting on the principle of double affect.

The next moral principle is known as "Epekia." I acted on this principle more than once when I was in a very complex or complicated situation. The principle of Epekia is far-reaching, and requires those who use it to research each situation. This is a call for discernment, and the motivation of love and compassion to act in the best interest for any situation. Using the principal of Epekia requires a high degree of maturity, wisdom and love, knowing that when news becomes public there can be criticism from those unaware of the principle of Epekia.

The third principle is referred to as the "Internal Form" for marriages. The internal form is similar to confession whereby there is no paper to be signed, and occurs when a couple who love each other desire to have their marriage blessed by the Church. They would not have obtained a declaration of nullity. This internal form for the blessing of a marriage, is truly of the Church and makes for a valid marriage. Over the years I often ask people to keep it quiet, because I know that the public at large is not aware of the internal form for the blessing of marriages, when there is lack of a declaration of nullity. However, this is a solid Catholic teaching, and the internal form for a valid marriage is just as real as any other form. Today as I reflect on this, I think of all the couples - and there have been many - who have taken advantage of this internal form and had loving and happy marriages. Unfortunately many Priests do not know about this Church legislation, and as a result tell people there is nothing they can do for them. This is not true. If you have any questions, I suggest you google "internal form for Catholic marriages." You will see that there is a vast amount of material available on the topic.

These three principles, or tools, are used very often in pastoral ministry. I am grateful for knowing them, and for having been taught them by progressive Priests. I have been able to minister to many hundreds of people in a creative and caring pastoral manner, in order to further their love for each other and assist in their happiness.

Also, by applying these three principles to various everyday situations, many people have been able to experience the Church as hospitable, caring and compassionate. It left them with the feeling that they do belong to a caring Church. This is the kind of Church Jesus would have wanted. Jesus was a man of compassion and kindness, and always willing to assist. It is my sense that the Catholic Church needs to be reformed in order to become more relevant, to be more like Jesus. The Church needs to be welcoming, provide comfort, and exercise the kind of pastoral care that brings people closer to God and not further away. I have seen some clergy who are more strict than the Church, and as a result people have been hurt.

People have not received compassionate pastoral care, and have walked away. They did not lose their faith in God - they lost their faith in the Church that had let them down. I thank God that I learned these moral principles, because they enabled me to put people first, rules and regulations second, and to know that I was doing the right thing. Today, as I look back over the years and am coming to the end of my journey, my deep gratitude is to the two Priests from Buffalo who came to St. Augustine Seminary so long ago. They taught me moral principles that enabled me to do pastoral care in a manner I never imagined. The fact that they only remained for two years, makes me question if they left on their own accord or were terminated? I will never know.

I remember that dealing with the authority of the day was my number one burden. I would never apologize, because in my mind and heart I was being true to God by putting people first. Secondly, whenever it was suggested that I stop doing something that was helpful to people, I would simply say, "Oh sure, I will do that," and yet I knew I would not change. Change would have required me to refuse to help people. Living out the promise I made to God has been a rewarding experience. It has also cost me dearly. I have lost the friendships of clergy and laity who did not understand, or know why I was doing what I was doing.

Towards the end of my active ministry, when I was baptizing more children than all the parishes in the city, I was refused, by several pastors, the use of their Church as well as Mount St. Joseph. Did it hurt? Yes. However, many years ago I learned a good lesson. Never take offence at the actions of others, or you will lose your inner peace. When I made the decision not to take offence, I knew that I would always preserve my tranquility. I valued that, above the resentment or bitterness of others. The only prayer I make these days is, "Thank you God for constantly inspiring me to be true to myself, true to the teachings of Jesus, and as often as I can, to offer caring pastoral ministry." As I complete my life's journey, I am so grateful for the experience of priesting all the people of God, with no exclusions. Deo Gratias

Chapter 25

THE CHURCH REBORN

My memories of the role of the Church start with St. Paul's Parish in Norwood, Ontario. My father died accidentally, and left my mother with the sole responsibility of managing our farm business. The sudden death of my father was a terrible shock to my mother. She needed courage and strength to carry on, as there were seven of us still at home, and a business to manage. She was the parish organist, which earned her 25 cents per Mass.

My mother was a woman of deep strong faith, and she drew on her trust in God to strengthen her to manage and face her responsibilities. The first thing I remember, is that she kept us on our knees to pray the rosary every evening, with her list of intentions. She was faithful to her Sunday Mass no matter how long it was, and God was a daily dessert in our home. For example, she offered grace before and after meals. She set the tone and we all learned from that powerful example. As I look back, I see that all my siblings were Church-attending people their entire life.

Pastoral Reflection

The history of my family is a microcosm of the Church down through the ages. I think of the millions of people who have found hope and meaning in the Church. I think of the thousands of pastors, who like our pastor visited my mother to comfort her in her grief.

We need balanced thinking when we go to Church. Dualistic thinking only sees one side of the equation, whereas non-dualistic thinking considers both sides. So the Church is both light and dark, good and bad. Those living in the light need to know and see the Church's shadow as well as the good that has been accomplished - then and now - and especially by the laity and religious women.

For example, the dedication of the Church toward education. Over the centuries the initiative and creativity of the religious orders of women has been incredible, to provide schools for children. Eventually these Sisters opened up universities as well. With good education, lives and career opportunities flourished. Religious orders of men like the Jesuits, continue to be busy in the field of education.

Later when parishes built parish schools, they were staffed by Sisters, and then lay women and men, as the model continues today. Then healthcare became a top priority of the Church. Catholic men and women attended medical school and became doctors. Catholic-run hospitals were built and staffed, and the population at large were offered expert health care. Poor people were never turned away, and all were welcome.

I recall the manner in which the people of the Church reached out to communities at large, to the poor and marginalized. In our own time we have seen courageous people inspired with a desire for social justice move into the public eye, in order to challenge racism, discrimination against LGBTQ community, poverty and violence. They have set an example for all of us to follow. This is just a small sampling of the activities of the people of the Church.

Historians maintained that when the Roman Empire collapsed, ordinarily the state religion would as well. Not so with Christianity. Once a civic official informed me, that the contribution of the Churches of the city to civic life saved the city thousands of dollars.

My own feeling is that the Church is old-fashioned, but is still my Mother and I love her. In the face of this, I have maintained my freedom to remain a practicing Catholic, knowing that she has a huge shadow.

It is my hope that by moving from dualistic to non-dualistic thinking, we will claim the good that Church people are doing. Hopefully we will be able to appreciate what is known as the Holy Spirit Guides, and inspire people to create a Church that is relevant to the 21st century. I hope and pray that the Church will be reborn in some new shape and form.

Deo Gratias

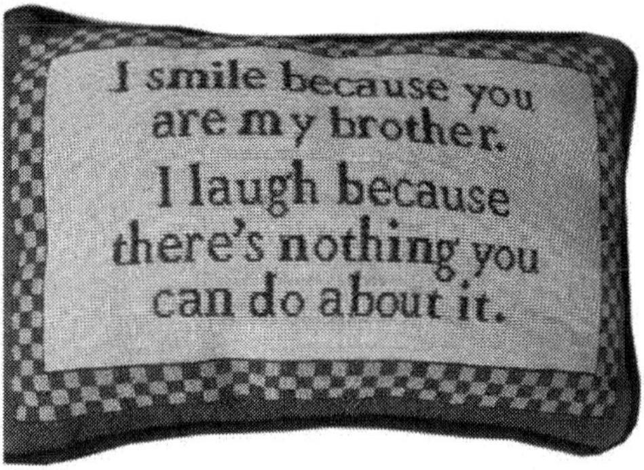

To my dear brother, Father Leo
From your beloved sister Shirley

Chapter 26

THE FUTURE OF OUR CHURCH

When I was ordained to the Priesthood in 1958, I began my ministry as an ordained Priest with enthusiasm and zeal. My original thought was that I just needed to carry on as things had been for 500 years, and keep things moving in the same direction. There was a generation of Priests on whose shoulders I stood. These were men who had given their life to the service of the Church, good Church men. I admired these men, was inspired by them, and learned a great deal about ministry from them. That generation of Irish Priests was a real blessing for me.

Then there was my own generation of Priests. Young men ordained a few years ahead of me, and a few years after me. We were the gang who studied the documents of Vatican Council II. For several years we met every Friday evening, going through the documents. We were excited. We felt a whole new energy vibrating in the Church, and we were faced with the task of implementing Vatican II.

Then things started to go sideways, as several of the young Priests decided on other careers. Suddenly there were fewer of us left. However, we continued to move forward.

Then one day we all woke up, and realized that the energy of the Vatican Council II had dissipated. Vatican II was no longer vibrant or alive in the Church. A generation of new Priests followed me - dedicated, enthusiastic, devoted Priests. Looking back, I can see that somehow events in the wider world were sucking energy out of the Church. People were no longer believing in our 500-year-old Faith Story. A generation of educated, critical thinkers no longer believed the dogma and doctrine. They wanted freedom, and not to be controlled by the clergy. They began to show this with their feet, walking away first by the hundreds and then by the thousands. For these past years, it is primarily older people in the pews on Sunday morning, and even these numbers are dwindling.

I meet so many of what I call "used to be" Catholics in our city. Caring and kind people, who can no longer swallow the 500-year-old faith story that is built on a three-tier universe, built on original sin and other kinds of sin. A system in which people are called sinners, and live in fear of being judged by a punitive God who would send them to purgatory or hell. This is a God of conditional love, a God of law and requirements, and the Church is there to enforce the laws of God. The emphasis is on orthodoxy and not orthopraxi. It seems to me that the Church wants to control people and their lives. Pelvic morality seems to be the main sermon preached from the pulpit, and people feel sinful about their sexual life. People live with fear and guilt. When I journey with people preparing to die, the fear of death comes to the surface. It is not so much a fear of dying, it is the fear of judgment and punishment from an authoritarian God. As I look at it now, it is no wonder millions of Catholics here in North and South America have walked away from the institutional Church. Many predict that our religion will go extinct, or simply followed by only a few numbers. Who knows?

Even so, it looks as if the institutional Church is dying. Yet we know that when there is an ending, there is always a new beginning. I see a new awakening happening in the world.

One characteristic of this new awakening is that people want spirituality and not religion. Many of the people who have quit religion have opted for spirituality. For some the choice of spirituality is primarily the rejection of organized religion. For others, there is a sincere desire to grow their spirituality, to grow in their union with God, themselves, all people, the world and all of creation. To do this, there must be practices offered to nurture the growth of people's spirituality.

It is not only Church people who are seeking spirituality, but also many others, who seek a spirituality that gives them meaning, and a purpose in life larger than themselves. We live in a postmodern world where evolution is exploding in every area - space travel, computers, cell phones, smart phones, artificial intelligence, robots, drones, e-cars, education, spirituality, politics, and economic systems.

Does An Institution have a Future?

The Church cannot continue to offer people a "prepackaged God." We have done this for 500 years, and it is no longer viable in the 21st century. Evolution is a reality and there is no denying it. Science like physics, quantum physics, quantum mechanics, string theory, biology, artificial intelligence, and new cosmology (to name a few important sciences) are what the clergy must become familiar with, and leave behind the prepackaged God. Knowing that people are searchers and seekers, religion must bring to people the experience of the evolutionary God, who is moving all of creation - including humans - into the future. God has a project which is to bring about the Kingdom of God, a world of love and justice for all humankind. The static world of the past no longer exists. A static religion of the last 500 years is dead in the water. Admit it.

As a friend of mine once said, "When you find you are riding a dead horse get off it." The seminary training of future Priests has to be radically updated, if they are going to be of any help to people transitioning into the future. As a species we are a future species, not of the past, or even the present.

If we are the Christian Church and do not show leadership, then obviously people will turn to other leaders who are providing spiritual leadership that makes sense, seems real, is more relevant, and helps people become fully alive and human. As people become fully alive, they will be inspired by the Spirit to do God's work, and commit themselves to build the Kingdom of God on Earth. They will be spirit people inspired by, and transformed by, the spirit and will carry in their heart the fire of the spirit. They will accomplish great things - even more than Jesus did. As a Christian people we have lost so much, by ignoring the Holy Spirit for far too long. And without the Holy Spirit we are simply a human-driven organization, relying on programs to do good. That is not it.

As I close out this chapter I do so with hope and optimism. I am reminded of the song, "The spirit is moving all over this land." Jesus said that the Spirit is like the wind that blows where it will, and this is so true. In my own lifetime, over and over again I have experienced the promptings of the spirit, which brings me words or actions that contribute to the well-being of people. Back in the 70's and 80's we had a charismatic renewal, and it transformed the lives of thousands of people around the world. After a few years we went back to the "same old same old." The Church has become stagnant, static and irrelevant.

One day I was talking to a United Church Minister and he said, "Father Leo, the problem with Catholic clergy is that you are dualistic thinkers, which is not much use in the 21st century." I said to him, "What is a dualistic thinker?" He replied, "A dualistic thinker thinks in terms of either/or, right/wrong, good/sinful, white/black, in/out, and it is the thinking that separates people." He continued, "In your Church that claims to be the one true Church, everyone else is outside, and yet we are all members of the Body of Christ. If we are going to follow Jesus and His teachings, we have to learn to live with ambiguity, which is the reality of life." I asked him, "What kind of thinking are you talking about?" He replied, "Non-dualistic thinking, when you are able to think in terms of both/and, this/that, light/dark, and in/out.

People who think non-dualistically are able to live with, and see the ambiguities of life, and hold the ambiguities with intention and achieve integration and growth. Non-dualistic thinking enables us to live with ambiguity and exclude no one, and therefore the inclusions of the gospel are possible." Then he said to me, "You Catholics are famous for excluding people. You exclude Protestants, you exclude Catholics who are divorced, you exclude your own women, you exclude Catholics who do not have a declaration of nullity and wish to be married, you exclude gay and lesbian people, you exclude people of colour, and you even end up calling your own people sinners and threatening them with hell and damnation. All of this and much more is against the teachings of Jesus. The other aspect of having been taught dualistic thinking, is that many of your people are living with guilt and fear, as they are controlled by binary thinking. You may not like to hear it, but it is the truth, and if you can swallow the truth, it can set you free."

I went home angry at his words. However, I had learned to sit and listen to my anger. I pondered the situation prayerfully, and then I realized that he was right and I was wrong. I had to change my thinking, in order to assume the mind of Christ. I did change my way of thinking. I came to be able to live in comfort with ambiguity, and practice inclusivity to all people. The United Church Minister was an amazing grace for me. One of the most important teachings of Jesus is "Metanoia" - that is, to change your thinking. This was a powerful transformative moment for me, and I always thank God for the words of that United Church Minister who was so right. Our Church has a long history of judging people based on who is right and who is wrong, or who gets excommunicated. Even now sexism runs rampant in our Church, and women are forbidden to be ordained just because they are female. This is a ridiculous situation, that is maintained by men in the Vatican who still think dualistically.

Old Bishops are still trying to control the Catholic people of the world, and they will never change unless they follow Jesus and change their thinking.

I suggest that you pay no attention to anything that comes out of the Vatican. Lately the Edict has come out from the Vatican forbidding Priests to officiate at same-sex marriages. I announced very clearly that I would willingly officiate at any same-sex marriage at any time. When the Vatican issued the Humana Vitae, an encyclical on artificial birth control, that statement was totally wrong, and went against the majority vote on the commission. On that day the Vatican lost all moral authority in the world. The Church does not have any place in the bedroom of the nation, especially a group of old men - Priests, Bishops and Cardinals - who are supposed to be celibate and yet, for the most part, are very sexually active. Give me a break!

The rebuilding of the Church will not come from the top. It is too corrupt, and too unfaithful to Jesus. A new Church will be built by the humble, the marginalized, the poor and the oppressed. If you do not agree with me, then read the gospel and see what Jesus said about this. You are called to join in as a friend of Jesus, and rebuild His Church just like St. Francis did. It is your decision and your answer, to the God who loves you and calls you by name.

Deo Gratias

Chapter 27

THE FINAL CHAPTER

As I sit here tonight, I am reflecting on, and pondering the 64+ years of my pastoral ministry. I remember back in the 70's, many of my classmates were leaving the Priesthood. Some people asked me if I was going to leave as well. Not being a very polite person, I said, "I won't let the bastards drive me out of my Church!" In spite of what some people think, I committed myself to the Church many years ago, and did not change my mind. My love for the Catholic Church has never wavered.

Yes, I came to the conclusion that the Church was missing its mark, with corrupt leadership that failed to see the changing times. A Church that closed ranks, and insisted on preaching and teaching the "same old same old" while expecting different results. I saw that evolution was changing everything. Einstein said that to keep doing the same thing and expect a different result, was a sign of insanity. I saw that while I loved the Church, my first love and loyalty was to God. So in ministering to people, I followed the example of Jesus, who often acted above the law to show compassion for people. Jesus taught and lived love.

I remembered the Spirit telling me at my first Mass to put people first, before rules, regulations or tradition. My conscience is, and always has been at peace, and being reprimanded was just a bump in the road. As I reflect on my journey, I see the presence and love of God manifest. In so many people I saw the presence of God - in the walking wounded, and in those finding life difficult and experiencing much pain. Their pain became my pain, and their suffering made room for me to enter and love.

I soon saw that I needed to be a competent Priest. So I decided to return to Ottawa University, study psychology and become a professional counselor to add to my ministry. This was the best decision I could have made. I attended a clinic in Philadelphia, to learn a model for inner healing and the healing of memories. As a result of combining psychology and healing prayer, I was able to minister to many people. I did not do this to make money, as I did not charge a large stipend and the people who came for counselling were not rich. With all the other dimensions of ministry (and there are multiple), I certainly enjoyed being a therapist, and to see people more fully alive and free to live their life to the fullest. It was gratifying. I always knew that it was the grace of God that brought about the healing and transformation.

The question remains, if I came back to Earth a second time, would I be a Priest-Therapist again? This is a rhetorical question. But after 64 years of ministry, I have to say I look back with a certain amount of gratification and accomplishment. I am overwhelmed with the amount of gratitude I have received over the years, and this I so very much appreciate. There were difficult times, especially when I received hate mail - and I did get my share. Through all this, I saved myself by not taking offence, knowing that if I did the only person I would hurt would be myself. There were so many people who loved and trusted me, that I often wondered if they realized how fragile I was. For all the people who made up my spiritual family, I thank you from the bottom of my heart. You taught me, you inspired me, you forgave me, you loved and supported me.

In my life, spiritual directors made a tremendous difference. People need a spiritual director to help them grow, and deepen and strengthen their relationship with God. To my real family - my parents, my seven sisters and three brothers I say, “Thank you,” for all the love and support you have given me over the years.

As I close this chapter of my book, I am grateful and humble that the God of the universe called me to love and serve His people. I am a country boy, and I always knew where I came from and who I am. Life has been an adventure, full of surprises, laughter and joy, along with grief and pain. I see the exit sign at the end of the road of life. When Sister Death comes calling I will answer, “Yes, it is time.” As I see it, I will shift from being a three-dimensional being, to enjoy living as a two-dimensional person. I wonder what it will be like! I wonder about the possible surprises.

Deo Gratias

Afterword

A CATHOLIC MANIFESTO

MYSTICAL EXPERIENCES

It began for me when I was about ten years old, and for some reason I simply followed my instinct. In Chapter 15 I talk about the grove of tall pine trees where I made my chapel. It was so beautiful there, with a little stream flowing past. The chipmunks played, bees buzzed, the birds sang and there was the whisper of the wind in the treetops. I just sat there. I had never heard the scripture, "Be still and know that I am God." This was my first mystical experience.

My next mystical experience happened while riding on a tractor and cultivating a field. As I drove the tractor back and forth across the land, I was somewhere else. I don't know where, but I felt as though I was transported to God.

My next mystical experience came on the top of Mount Tremblant. It was on a beautiful cold winter day in February. I got off the chair lift at the top of the mountain, and decided to stop and look out as far as the eye could see. Something happened to me. Again, I was transported. When I came back to Earth, all I know is that I said to God, "Take me now I am ready to go!"

My next mystical experience was after high school. I heard God calling me to the Priesthood night after night until finally I said "Yes." I registered at St. Augustine's Seminary in Toronto and completed the seven years of study. My next mystical experience came on a Sunday morning when I was celebrating my first Mass. As we started to say the Apostles Creed, I heard the voice of God within me say, "Father Leo, I want you to always put people first." Naturally I had no idea what I was supposed to do, but I knew that I would always put people first, because that was what God had asked me to do.

After five years of ministry I discovered that I was working in a very legalistic institution called the Catholic Church. There were many rules and regulations that allowed Priests to deny God to people, especially in the area of marriage. In Chapter 13 I talk about a young woman coming to me for help, so she and her fiancé could be married in the Church. We did the Internal Form which is a valid Church marriage, and I married them.

When the news got out, soon many people were coming to me asking if I would officiate at their second marriage. I never turned anyone away, and from this I learned the meaning of the words, "Put my people first." Now here I am, an old man of 90 looking back through the rearview mirror, reflecting on my life and my experiences.

As I bring this work to completion I want to quote one of my favorite authors Brian McLaren, author of the book *The Great Spiritual Migration* (Convergent Books, 2016). He says that the pattern is predictable. Founders are typically generous, visionary, bold and creative, but the religion that ostensibly carries on their work often becomes the opposite - constricted, change-adverse, fearful, nostalgic, obsessed with boundary maintenance, turf battles and money.

Instead of greeting the world with open arms as their founders did, they are successors standing guard with clenched fists. Instead of empowering others as their founders did, they hoard power.

Instead of defying tradition and unleasing moral imagination as their founders did, they oppose tradition and refuse to think outside the lines. A religion that cuts itself off from the example of its founder, and while still bearing the founder's name, often becomes little more than a chaplaincy for other ideologies, offering its services to the highest bidder. No wonder so many religious folks today wear down, burn out and opt out.

No wonder more and more of us who are Christians by birth, or by choice, find ourselves shaking our heads and asking, "What happened to Christianity? What happened to Jesus and His beautiful message?" What is the Church really about? I've always understood the Church to be a community with a shared story in the scriptures that bind us together. Church is about weaving relationships, so that life for all of us is more deeply rooted in love. Today I would maintain that the Church also offers a platform to work together, to build a world that acts and advocates for the common good of all. We are warriors, lovers, peacemakers, protectors, prophets, thinkers, and dreamers who gather together to celebrate our heritage as children of God.

At the same time, we are fearlessly willing to stand up for those of our culture who are oppressed. We have an opportunity in this moment of our great transformation. We can approach this time as survivors, desperately clinging to our structures and ways of being. Or, we can see ourselves as pioneers setting out in the face of the unknown to discover new ways to live faith-filled lives. The inevitable decline of our structures gives us a chance to let go of what might hold us back from that adventure. Nothing today will be the same ten years from now. Why not architect the kind of faith movement we want to see 20 or 50 years from now? What do we have to lose?

Following Brian McLaren's statement, I now put forth my own idea of how we might move toward the future Church. First, I envision how the Church of the future has already birthed a "Parallel Church."

It is important that the Parallel Church is the movement within the institutional Church, and not outside of it. This movement would be subversive, and due to a different type of leadership either bring Clericalism to an end, or convert and renew the universal Church. This parallel movement would be subversive to the institution and the power structure that has evolved down through the centuries.

A leadership in the Parallel movement would be lay-driven. Here I refer to the Priesthood of the laity, which could include married and single men and women, who are truly dedicated to washing the feet of the people. These people in leadership would be chosen and approved by the people. The present model of creating ordained Priests for generation after generation will disappear. There may or may not be ordained people in the Priesthood. But if a woman or man indicates that they have been called into the Priesthood, the faith community will decide whether or not they are appropriate, and also decide on how such a person will be trained.

The parallel movement is always future-oriented and in step with the evolution in the world. I would imagine that after 500 years, it too would need a subversive movement and disappear. Human nature being what it is, the inclination for prestige and power will not go away. I see that the reform and conversion of the Universal Church must come from the power in the force of the Body of Christ, and not from a distant clerical power. There is always resistance to any kind of renewal, or the letting go of power to control.

This is my vision for the possible renewal of the Church that is true to its purpose - which is to bring about the Kingdom of God in the hearts of people, and to live and preach a message of good news that will give people hope and meaning in their lives. Above all, it must be relational for all the people of the world.

It is not an institution but a movement.

The birthed new Church is Spirit-empowered.

I see the new Church coming into existence as people gather for bible study, faith sharing, justice work, loving and protecting the environment, different outreaches to the poor and homeless, peace-making, nonviolence work, equality for women and the LGBTQ community. All are equal and integral to the life of the new Church. In other words, "All are welcome no one is turned away." In my writing on clericalism and what is happening in the world, to the people of God I say that clericalism is obsolete and must disappear. This will happen as the parallel Church becomes an ever-increasing movement in many parts of the world. The institutional Church is short on money, and as the parallel Church grows and fewer people attend the Church buildings, money will become a real issue for those who are corrupt and living a double life.

However, that is not the problem of those choosing the parallel Church. I do foresee the day when the clergy living a double life will be in a museum; a piece of history of what once was. I do hope that my story encourages some to say yes to belonging to the parallel Church. It is already birthed! I see the parallel Church as being a new form of democracy. The Priesthood of the laity will flourish, leaders will be chosen by the community, and if there evolves an ordained Priestly ministry it will include women or men, single or married. I believe that at this time in history God is doing a "New Work." The Body of Christ is rising from the ashes, and the Jesus story is safe. It will be lived and told for many generations to come, perhaps for 500 or 1000 years. And then it will die and rise again. The Pascal Mystery is a lived experience by the people of God, and today we have the opportunity to make it happen again.

Such is my manifesto.

Deo Gratias

Deo Gratias

About the Author

Fr. Leo Coughlin was born into a family of eleven children and grew up on a 500-acre dairy farm near Norwood, Ontario. He was ordained to the Priesthood in 1958, and several years later returned to university to obtain a Masters Degree in Pastoral Counseling. During his ministry years he was Director of Adult Education and facilitator for pre-marriage courses, and focused on parish work, spirituality seminars and retreats, and the practice of psychotherapy. He has also been actively involved in the community with Big Brothers, sports and recreation. In his later years he continued on in ministry as a Faith Animator in the Catholic School System, and as chaplain to the Sisters of St. Joseph. Fr. Leo has embraced technology as a means of connecting with people, and offers the live-streaming of Sunday mass. He also teaches meditation and gathers people on Zoom for the discussion of relevant topics. He is a life-long student, feeling that as a Priest he needs to be competent and up-to-date in regard to spirituality and the "new story" that combines science and faith, in order to be more relevant in the world. Fr. Leo has his own website, (www.leospot.ca) and has posted his popular "Thought for the Day" in recent years on social media. His first book, *Daily Reflections: Arising from Silence and Solitude* is a collection of those writings. In all of his published work, Fr. Leo hopes that readers will find inspirations for daily living, and for meeting the many challenges we face today.

Manufactured by Amazon.ca
Bolton, ON

26283600R00077